The Protein-Powered Vegetarian

The Protein-Powered Vegetarian

From Meat to Vegetable Protein

A Cookbook with Spirit

Bo Sebastian

iUniverse.com, Inc.
San Jose New York Lincoln Shanghai

The Protein-Powered Vegetarian
From Meat to Vegetable Protein

All Rights Reserved © 2000 by Bo Sebastian

No part of this book may be reproduced or transmitted in any form or by any
means, graphic, electronic, or mechanical,including photocopying, recording,
taping, or by any information storage retrieval system, without the
permission in writing from the publisher.

Published by iUniverse.com, Inc.

For information address:
iUniverse.com, Inc.
5220 S 16th, Ste. 200
Lincoln, NE 68512
www.iuniverse.com

ISBN: 0-595-13274-X

Printed in the United States of America

Acknowledgements

My sincerest thanks go to my agent, James Schiavone, for his help and support with my literary career. I also owe a debt of gratitude to Michael Manly for his constant encouragement; to Kimberly, Linda, Amy, Paul, Ed, Faith, Joanna, and Tameron for friends to lean on; to my family, from whom most of these recipes got their origin; to my sister, Lori, for helping me with my first cookbook at age eight; to Mom and in memory of my dad for giving me wings to fly; and to God for blessing me with this beautiful life.

Contents

Introduction

For ten of my forty years, I swung back and forth from carnivore to vegetarian. While I was free of meat, my body felt as if it were severely lacking protein at a cellular level. At worst, I felt my body scream out for a hamburger or a steak! Sometimes I gave into my cravings and convinced myself that humans are inherently carnivores.

Now I sincerely believe that all my cravings for meat truly had been a hunger for protein, as I had assumed a vegetarian diet replete with all vegetables and complex carbohydrates and an occasional bout of beans and nuts. I ended up pear-shaped and much heavier than I wanted to be, even though I ate what appeared to be an extremely healthy diet. Again, I returned to meat for three years.

Five years ago, though, I decided to return to vegetarianism—this time with the understanding I needed to remain healthy and protein sufficient. In the market today, you find vegetarian protein products assimilating pork—in the form of vegetarian bacon and sausage; beef—in the form of vegetarian ground beef and burgers and seitan, which looks like tenderloin; turkey- and ham-style deli slices; hot dogs; and even pepperoni and salami. The great news: Most vegetarian products are fat free.

For many years I had no idea that vegetables were carbohydrates. A normal human body can only process so many carbohydrates before it begins turning even those precious edible plants to cellulite.

Too many carbohydrates and too little protein cause dietary problems.

As a vegetarian on a high protein diet, I feel deprived of nothing. I eat normal, ethnic, and American foods using the many new meat-free products now in the marketplace.

My intention in this book is to help you find vegetarian protein products to substitute for the meat in all the wonderful ethnic and traditional American foods you once ate. Also, I would like to assist you in finding herbs and spices to make these foods taste absolutely delicious. We deserve nothing less.

Chapter 1

The Shopping List

My family generally planned meals around meat: pot roast with mashed potatoes and carrots, pork chops with fried potatoes and canned corn, meatballs and spaghetti, or hamburgers and French fries. At our dinner table meat took the throne; a starch in the form of potatoes, rice, or pasta supplied the remainder of the court. If I were lucky, as a child I may have gotten fresh broccoli at Christmas, or garden vegetables in the summer. But most of the time, we ate canned vegetables—over-cooked, canned vegetables—with the life force sucked right out of them.

This book should help you settle on an interesting main course, which will often include various vegetable protein sources. You, then, will combine your protein with energizing fresh vegetables. And yes, you may even digress and add some of the more tempting pastas and complex carbohydrates that you crave so often. But these you will eat in small doses.

The key here: You must proportion your protein, carbohydrate, and fat intake. Many high-protein diets suggest an over abundance of carbohydrates—especially complex carbohydrates, such as breads, potatoes, and pasta—can lead to gaining excess weight and eventually heart disease. One of these diets suggests the proper ratio of protein to carbohydrates to fat is 30-40-30. This ratio supposedly keeps your insulin levels stable, where you will have the most energy and assimilate food efficiently. The Food and Drug Administration (FDA) advocates a 20% protein and 80% carbohydrate diet. My diet is somewhere in between the FDA and the 30-40-30 diet, as I have never been legalistic.

We only need to look around at the supermarkets and malls to see that Americans are overweight. Our diet standards simply do not work. I do not say this to be cruel. I exclaim it, so people will wake up to this fact and begin to change their unhealthy diet habits. I do not even care if you become a strict vegetarian. My hope is to give you alternatives—new options and recipes; then, let you decide.

Discovering Meat-free Textures

Below is a partial list of vegetarian protein, most of which you can buy at your local grocery. At Kroger in Nashville, for example, consumers find some products in the vegetable department and some in the frozen foods next to the breakfast foods. If you cannot find a product in your local grocery, try your neighborhood health food stores. The national chain, Wild Oats, has just about every vegetarian product available.

Tofu

Tofu contains high levels of protective plant-based chemicals shown to be highly protective against cancer. It specifically prevents breast and endometrial cancer in women and prostate cancer in men. Tofu also helps reduce cholesterol levels and subsequent heart disease risk in both men and women. To receive the maximum benefits from soy, adults should consume about six to ten ounces of tofu daily, equivalent to one very low-calorie meal.

One day I tasted Italian-baked tofu and thought I was eating my dad's broiled chicken. Honestly.

When I first tried tofu, I have to say I did not like it, basically because of its gelatinous texture. It had little taste, and I maintain that to this day. However, its texture can be changed by baking and frying it, which removes most of its water and leaves it tougher and chewier.

Tofu is a flavor chameleon, taking on the spices and herbs of whatever it is near. Tofu can have many different kinds of textures. I can bet if you tried each of them, you would not even know some were tofu. For example, when I serve lasagna, I mix ricotta and Romano cheeses with tofu. By doing this, I added a major source of protein to a pasta dish. No one ever knows.

Five ounces of tofu give you twenty-one grams of protein. This varies according to which tofu you choose. That means you get three servings per sixteen ounce container. At most Oriental grocery stores, you can find tofu from 50¢ to $1.29 a container. Do not pay more at your local grocery chain. *Hinoichi* brand, which is considered by most Asians in my community to be top of the line, is only $1.29 at the Chinese grocery. But most tofu is $1.79 or above at the local grocery. Also, you can buy reduced fat tofu now. I recommend it.

I love to find a bargain. Do yourself a favor and check out your city's Farmer's Market or your local Asian or MidEastern Global Market. You will not be sorry.

Marinated Baked Tofu

If you want to use tofu in place of beef or chicken, you may consider marinating and baking it. This recipe will provide a chewy texture with a nutty flavor.

RECIPE

Simply cut tofu into half-inch slices and marinate them in a half cup soy sauce or a quarter cup Bragg Liquid Aminos overnight. If you are in a hurry, an hour will do. In preparation for baking, coat tofu slices with a thick layer of nutritional or Brewers yeast.

Place on a cookie sheet sprayed with olive oil non-stick cooking spray. Bake at 350° for 30-45 minutes. If you want to make your slices thicker, bake at a lower temperature for a longer period of time. The longer you bake them, the more they becomes like jerky.

Concerned about yeast in your diet? Nutritional and Brewers yeast will not grow in your body like the yeast in bread. It provides trace minerals and vitamins rarely found in other foods and is rich in protein, having 7 grams per tablespoon of Brewers and 4 grams per tablespoon for nutritional yeast. The difference between the two: Brewers yeast is grown on beet molasses; nutritional yeast is grown on cane and beet molasses.

I sometimes snack on cold, crispy baked tofu. It is a wonderful protein-enriched extra to keep in the refrigerator to add to almost any of your favorite meals.

Remember: Add the proper amount of protein to your diet so your food metabolizes efficiently.

Fried Tofu

Most people drain the water from tofu by placing it in a colander or tofu strainer for an hour. Otherwise, you can put slices between two small saucers and press them together over a sink. I admit, most of the time, I use neither method.

RECIPE
Depending on how fat conscious you are, you can add olive oil to a frying pan and preheat it on medium-high heat. Then, simply fry chunks of tofu until they become golden brown.

If you want tofu to take on the texture of cooked chicken, cut tofu into long, thin strips and fry it for approximately twenty minutes on medium low heat, browning it slowly. Remember: The longer you cook tofu, the chewier it becomes.

At this point, we have not flavored the fried tofu, so the taste remains bland. These initial techniques help prepare tofu for its texture, not flavor. The use of herbs comes next.

Scrambled Tofu

You can crumble tofu and use it like scrambled eggs, cooking it gently until it becomes hot. We'll make one of my favorite scrambled tofu dishes called *Tiger Food* later in the book.

Uncooked Tofu

I have only one recipe for uncooked tofu, but it is excellent in place of egg salad and has almost the same texture, but a more robust flavor. You will love it!

Soft Tofu

Soft tofu is used mostly for desserts. I have used it in my manicotti recipe, as well. It reminds me of gelatin and can be mixed with fresh fruit.

Seitan-Wheat Gluten

This meatlike texture looks and tastes much like either chicken or beef, depending on which version you buy. I have even seen fajita strips and sloppy Joe mix made with seitan. The brand I use is Upcountry, made in Pittsfield, Massachusetts, 01201. I make my own barbecue with it. The taste is wonderful. Seitan is incredibly high in protein, in fact, higher in protein than soy per ounce. I have also used this cut up in a stir-fry or with steamed vegetables. It has 3.75 grams of protein per ounce.

If making your own seitan interests you, buy wheat gluten at your local health food store and prepare it yourself with the simple recipe below. The homemade texture is less firm than store bought, but it is equally good.

RECIPE
(makes 3 cups seitan)

Mix thoroughly in a bowl:
1 cup instant gluten flour (vital wheat gluten)
7/8 cup water or vegetable stock (use herb broth, page 23)

Knead until blended. Divide into small, bite-size balls, stretching and pressing to flatten into cutlets.

Combine in a 4-5 quart sauce pot:
1/3 cup olive oil
2 sliced onions
1 clove garlic
1/2 cup brown sugar
3/4 cup soy sauce
6 cups water

Bring mixture to a boil. Drop the gluten cutlets into boiling stock and let simmer on low heat for 1 hour.

You can store this texture in the broth for up to a week in the refrigerator.

Morningstar Farms

Worthington Foods, Inc. manufacturers meat-free textures that simulate almost every meat. You can buy most of these products at your local grocery store in the freezer departments, usually next to the breakfast foods; however, these foods are under the Morningstar Farms brand name. The Worthington label is generally reserved for specialty stores. This company also provides a line of canned products like vegetarian pork chops and diced chicken.

Near my house in Nashville, we have a deluxe grocery which carries a variety of health food products in a special freezer by the ice cream. One day I noticed that the Worthington breakfast strips were exactly $1.10 more expensive under the Worthington trade label than the Morningstar Farms label. This is exactly the same product, made by the same company. Be aware. Specialty foods will cost you more, even in the same grocery store.

Hopefully, we can convince companies like Worthington that there is enough interest and buying power to attract more of their products to the mainstream Morningstar Farms label.

Below I have listed some of my favorite choices under this trade name.

Chik Nuggets, Meat-free Buffalo Wings, and Chik Patties

I have had countless clients tell me they successfully fooled their children into believing that the Chik Nuggets were chicken nuggets.

They really are tasty, but slightly high in fat. If it is a choice between the fat content in Chik Nuggets or fried chicken, you would be much better off with the soy product, which will give you thirteen grams of protein for every four nuggets.

Also, the Chik patties work well on a sandwich. It is simple and easy.

Try a little cheddar cheese—soy cheese, if you like—melted on the top with a dash of rubbed thyme and ground black pepper. Put this on a hard roll, and you will be set for a quick sandwich.

Spicy Black Bean Burgers

This burger, providing eleven grams of protein, does well with a Mexican fare. You can serve this with melted cheese and salsa and a side salad.

Breakfast Strips

When microwaved or fried, these strips taste so much like bacon, it even fools me. However, they only provide one gram of protein per strip and too many carbohydrates to add bread. The option here: create an egg or scrambled tofu sandwich with a couple pieces of Breakfast Strips for added flavor and protein. Also, try these with protein-fortified pancakes.

Grillers and Harvest Recipe

For texture and taste, this pseudoburger is one of the best on the market. The patty does not fall apart on the grill. It reminds me, though, of what a hamburger tasted like in my high school cafeteria days. One burger contains11 grams of protein. Take my advise, though, and dress it up with your favorite sandwich extras. The Harvest Recipe has twelve grams of protein per half cup and is used in place of ground beef.

Breakfast Links and Breakfast Patties

I have put these links in tomato sauce and fooled many carnivores. You can serve the links or patties with eggs, make a sandwich with them, and treat them as sausage.

Hot Dogs and Corn Dogs

I cannot tell the difference!

Yves Products

This Canadian company has won some awards for new business and definitely deserves them. They have come out with a line of fresh, in-your-produce-section, meat-free alternatives that will truly turn your head.

They are extremely expensive, but well worth it. And all their products are fat free!

Burgers

Yves premade burgers look and taste so much like beef, you may find it hard to distinguish them from real. One semester, a chef from a vegan restaurant in town tasted one in my cooking classes. After chewing it a few times, she kept the burger in her mouth while exclaiming, "I haven't had meat in ten years. Are you sure this is not hamburger?"

I prepare these burgers with a little Worcestershire sauce, a dash of McCormick Montreal Steak Seasoning, a dash of garlic powder, then top it off with cheese. They do well on the grill, as well. They have eleven grams of protein in each burger. Yves also makes an excellent ground round product to use in place of hamburger.

Veggie Pizza Pepperoni

It is been a long time since I have eaten pepperoni. Growing up in a traditional Italian family, you can be sure I had my share of salami and pepperoni. This fat-free alternative has made me a happy man.

Proportionately, cheese is a complete carbohydrate-protein-fat product. Up until recently, I had not been successful in getting the proper protein added to cheese and crackers to keep a 40-30-30 balance. Now the marriage is complete and tasty with Veggie Pepperoni.

This product has fourteen grams of protein per 2.5 ounces.

Canadian Bacon and Deli Slices

I have been using this product like ham slices. It has the texture of bologna, but not the extraneous animal parts. I make vegetarian Reuben sandwiches with these slices and have made some bored-with-their-food vegans happy campers. They have 16 grams of protein per three slices.

Veggie Wieners

I have to admit, these do not really taste, or feel, like hot dogs. I believe the Morningstar brand comes closest to the taste. For some, that is a good thing. For me, it is a nostalgic thing to have a hot dog with catsup, mustard, onions, cheese, or chili. These hot dogs are a fair substitute, in my estimation. They have 11 grams of protein.

These also come in a chili dog version, which definitely has more flavor.

Lightlife

Smart Deli Roast Turkey-style Slices

Melt a little butter with some onions and sauté a few fat free Deli Turkey-style Slices. Add a little Monterey Jack or mozzarella cheese and make an awesome, quick sandwich for lunch.

I bet this might be a good alternative for turkey in a packed lunch. Each slice contains three grams of protein.

Country Ham-style Slices

These slices are great on a Reuben sandwich. I make an Egg Beaters omelet with these slices. I also add cheddar cheese, tomato, onion, and pepper. These slices have ten grams of protein per three slices.

GardenBurgers

Made by Wholesome and Hearty Foods, Inc., these burgers come in a few varieties: Original, Hamburger style, and Hamburger style with cheese. I get bored with the same kinds of food all the time. So, a slightly different taste or flavor makes a world of difference. I especially like the cheese version.

The Original has only eight grams of protein, the hamburger style has twelve grams of protein, and the hamburger style with cheese has a whopping sixteen grams of protein per patty.

Hearty and Natural Products

This company makes a variety of prepared, microwave ready, dishes, such as Lemon Chicken-flavored patties and Teriyaki Chicken-flavored patties, which I think are excellent.

Loma Linda

My favorite item from this manufacturer is Corn Dogs. They are expensive, but great. They also have a line of canned protein products which I have not tried, as I am not much into canned food.

Boca Burgers

To my knowledge, there are few products out there that cater to the vegan lifestyle, which means no meat, as well as no dairy. There is a Boca Burger that is vegan.

Fantastic Foods Nature's Burger Mix

This powdered mix has been around for a long time. It is made of brown rice, dehydrated vegetables, barley, wheat, gluten flour, oats, sesame seeds, soy protein concentrate, dried yeast, and flavoring.

With all the new products on the market, this has become one of my least favorites. It is mealy and certainly will not last on the grill. You try it and see.

It contains seven grams of protein per one third cup.

Textured Vegetable Protein (TVP)

Before companies made meat-free products, vegetarians used TVP to replace meat. It comes in flakes, which can be used in chili and sauces and in large chunks and strips, which can be used in place of chicken or beef in many foods. Both versions must be hydrated. Quite often, I will throw the dried chunks or strips into tomato sauce and let them hydrate there, soaking up the flavor while they expand.

Like tofu, these products are virtually tasteless. If you use this texture to stir-fry, I recommend marinating them in a one-to-one combination of water and soy or teriyaki sauce first.

TVP flakes and chunks have twenty-four grams of protein per half cup.

Tempeh

Before all the different soy products came on the market, I was a big fan of tempeh. After careful study of vegetable protein, this is one of the least efficient in providing a high-protein, low-carbohydrate base. Tempeh is usually made with barley and brown rice, which already places it high on the carbohydrate list. Adding it to vegetables—more carbohydrates—does not make for a good protein-carbohydrate balance. It takes 1.5 ounces of tempeh to get seven grams of protein. I believe this varies according to what brand of tempeh you get.

If you enjoy the taste of tempeh, you can easily substitute it for Yves Veggie Ground Round or use it instead of the Canadian Bacon for the vegetarian Reuben. Use your imagination.

Beans

Old school thought was: a bean must be combined with a complex carbohydrate, rice, or pasta to make a complete protein. In books such as *Diet for a Small Planet*, Frances Moore Lappé originally expressed a need to combine beans with complex carbohydrates, but later recanted her claims. This subject has made its way into other vegetarian theory, and I will repeat it here: You do not need to combine beans with complex carbohydrates to get a complete protein. In their natural state beans are primarily a carbohydrate, but also contain protein. So be careful how many beans you eat.

If you prepare a bean or lentil soup, you probably have the proper proportion of protein to carbohydrate as is—without the barley or rice.

Cheese and Dairy

I still use dairy products, though many holistic practitioners say all dairy causes mucus in the digestive track and phlegm in the respiratory system.

If you are lactose-intolerant, soy cheese products exist on the market with about four grams of protein per slice. You can even buy pasta cheese, similar to Parmesan in a shaker jar, also made of soy.

If you are lactose-tolerant, milk products can be a wonderful way to supplement your diet with protein. Low fat milk and cheese have the perfect 40-30-30 balance of carbohydrate to protein to fat.

BIG MISTAKE! If you think you get enough protein in your breakfast diet simply by adding milk to your cereal in the morning, you are mistaken. Most boxed cereals have so little protein, you basically eat nothing but carbohydrates in the form of grains and sugars. Yes, even cereals that taste like they should be healthy are primarily protein deficient. If you combine that breakfast with coffee, I guarantee you will be hungry about an hour and half later.

Check out the suggestions for a protein-fortified breakfast later in the book.

Eggs

Plenty of vegetarians do not eat eggs. Egg substitutes are basically 99% egg whites and 1% egg yolk or coloring. I cannot even tell the difference.

Either way, eggs are high in protein and can be a great way to add a boost to your breakfast or lunch. They have seven grams of protein per egg or 6 grams of protein per quarter cup of egg substitute.

I stopped eating eggs because I did not want to eat an embryo that could have been a life. I discovered, though, that most commercial eggs are unfertilized. So, these eggs would never have been chickens. You actually have to go to a specialty store to buy fertilized eggs.

Nuts and Seeds

Nuts and seeds are also proteins but are considerably higher in fat. However, God put them on the earth, and I certainly enjoy eating a handful for a snack. Also, there are plenty of ways you can add nuts or nut butters to your meals. Some examples are: pine nuts in pesto, cashews in a stir-fry, and sesame seeds and sesame butter in cold sesame noodles and in Mediterranean fare. Most nuts have about ten grams of protein per one-quarter cup. This may vary according to the nuts. If you are susceptible to herpes simplex, you should watch out for eating too many nuts; they could cause an outbreak.

Chapter 2

Herbs and Spices—
Enhancing Your Food

As I discussed in chapter 1, vegetarian protein can be fairly bland. Therefore, understanding how to add herbs and spices to create the dish you desire becomes very important.

A complete novice at cooking should run down to a nearby world market grocery and buy some herbs and spices. Buying herbs in bulk by the ounce is much cheaper than buying even the generic grocery store brands. For instance, I found ten ounces of dill for $3.48 at a world market in Nashville. I priced one ounce of dill at my local supermarket for $3.99.

Buying the Basic Herbs and Spices

If I had to buy just a few herbs and spices, I would begin with these:

- *McCormick Grill Mates Montreal Steak Seasoning.* For a season-all that will enhance almost anything you make from burgers to sauces, this is the one to buy. It contains dill seed, coriander seed, black pepper, garlic, and paprika.

  I have recommended this—and the spicy hot version—to friends who have said it has changed their vegetarian food from boring to delicious.

- *Garlic.* You can buy dried garlic in a powdered form, minced, or enhanced with salt. My favorite version is freshly minced or chopped in a jar. It also comes as a juice and, of course, in its raw form. I keep garlic powder, the most intense dry version, in my pantry and also a jar of minced fresh garlic in my refrigerator. When I get industrious, I mince my own garlic in the food processor and store it in a jar covered in olive oil. If you want to become a cook or, at least, pretend you are one, garlic is a must.

- *Ginger.* You can buy ginger in a powder, freshly ground in a jar, or as a root. Personally, I buy ginger by the root, peel it, food process it, and then put it in a small jar covered with olive oil to protect it from aging. It will last about two months before growing mold.

- *Onion.* I use fresh onion most of the time, but in a pinch, onion powder or onion salt will do. Almost every culture uses onion for flavor. Vidalia onions are my favorite, because they are sweet and do not make you tear up when you chop them.

Here's a tip. Put an unpeeled onion in the microwave for one minute. When you peel it, you will not cry.

- *Sweet Basil.* Aromatic and intense, sweet basil can bring a salad, soup, or sauce to life. Fresh sweet basil tastes best, frozen comes second best, in a jar will do, and dried is my least favorite.

I grow sweet basil in the summer. (See Growing an Herb Garden on page 26) It is an annual herb, which means you must replant it every year. In the fall some varieties grow waist high, sprouting huge and beautiful leaves. At the end of the growing season, I harvest all the leaves, place them in a food processor with a little olive oil, and then freeze the pulp for use in the winter.

The trick to freezing any herb is to put the food-processed herb in a plastic freezer bag, seal it, then press it flat like a piece of cardboard, squeezing all the air out of the bag. This way, you can easily break off small, flat chunks for use in all fresh-basil recipes.

- *Parsley.* The Jewish culture considered this herb to be bitter, as it is their custom to eat a piece of parsley dipped in salt water at Passover. However, I think parsley has a wonderfully fresh taste. It is a beautiful garnish, as well, and can be used as a breath freshener after a meal. This is a perennial herb, usually lasting the entire winter in a temperate climate.
- *Cilantro.* If you are a salsa fan and enjoy Asian cooking, this herb is very important. However, you may have to acquire a taste for it. When I first tried it, I thought it tasted like soap. Now I cannot imagine cooking without it.
- *Dill.* If you have ever eaten a dill pickle, you have tasted this herb. Annually, it grows quickly and voluptuously by midJuly in Tennessee and must be harvested soon after. You must dry dill at that time. Tie the stalks together and hang them upside down in a dark, cool place. This will change its limp spines to crisp, green needles, easily dismembered from the stem by rubbing it between your palms.
- *Mint.* This prolific herb will take over your garden if you do not contain it in a pot. You can make herb tea and also tabouli with it.
- *Rosemary.* This is the last of the necessary herbs. Rosemary is a perennial. In most southern regions it can be nourished throughout the winter. I do not recommend taking it inside for the cold. During a bad snow, I would cover it. The part of the plant to use looks as if it were pine needles. If you have never smelled fresh

rosemary, you have missed a treasure. Every time I walk past my rosemary bush, I pluck off a needle and smell my hand. The flavor is equally delicious used in broth, potatoes, and in even in some pasta dishes.

Other Herbs to Have

- *Rubbed Thyme.* This herb is dried and pulverized to create a fine powder and compliments anything with cheese. Thyme reminds me of oregano, so it also adds a special flavor to salads. I often interchange the two spices. Similar to parsley, you can also buy thyme dried.
- *Oregano.* Used primarily in Italian cooking, this herb has a musty taste, familiar to most in pizza sauce. I usually grow this prolific herb; fresh, it is wonderful in tomato sauce and salads.
- *Tarragon.* This herb has always been difficult for me to grow in Tennessee. I have used it in some cream soups and French foods.
- *Sage.* You will remember the taste of this herb in bread stuffing. I grow this perennial herb and use it infrequently. But when I do, I always enjoy it.
- *Celery.* The reason I have put this in the not-so-necessary herbs is because I usually use fresh celery as a vegetable. You can, however, buy celery seed and celery juice. Nothing, of course, is better than fresh. Cooks primarily use celery in soups and salads.
- *Cinnamon.* I use cinnamon in my protein-fortified oatmeal almost every morning. Its rich, dark flavor brings this grain to life. It is also wonderful in breads and pastries.
- *Mustard.* I actually use dried mustard in cooking much more than the condiment and never use mustard seed. My favorite mustard as a condiment is Maille's A l'Ancienne old-style Dijon mustard. It is expensive, but the best I have ever tasted.

- *Coriander, Cumin, Curry, and Turmeric.* If you plan to cook any kind of Indian food, these are the primary dried spices.
- *Paprika.* This spice will taste like a mild pepper. Most health books consider it a stomach irritant, but I still use it.

I was told some years ago that most peppers, except cayenne, were stomach irritants. Recent research shows, though, all peppers are good for the stomach. The key here is: always eat what your body actually says it needs. You will not go wrong with this rule of thumb. Remember, too, that if you are prone to any urinary disorders, you may want to avoid peppers and the like.

- *Chives.* I always use fresh chives. In the summer, I grow them. In the winter I make a habit of buying the flowering chives at the local Chinese grocery; that is, if the winter is so cold my own die. Chopped, this herb is wonderful in soups, tomato sauces, or to garnish almost anything that would be enhanced by a mild onion flavor.

To keep chives fresh longer, chop and cover them with water in a small, sealed jar. In the refrigerator these chives will stay fresh and crunchy for the entire week. Just change the water every 2-3 days.

- *Nutmeg.* This dried spice reminds me of cinnamon. I use it mostly in cream sauces. I even like a little nutmeg in my macaroni and cheese.

For more information on spices and herbs, see the appendix.

Growing an Herb Garden

Preparing to grow an herb garden is like buying seasonings for your spice cabinet. First, you must decide what you need and what suits your palate. Check out your favorite recipes and decide what herbs you could grow in your climate.

Once you decide on the kinds of herbs you would like to grow:

- Choose which are annuals—you must replant each year—and which are perennials—they come back each year. In some climates perennials will continue to produce throughout the winter.
- Some plants hug the ground—such as oregano and thyme—and others grow as tall as adults—such as some dill varieties. Some take plenty of sun, others prefer shade.
- Some herbs flower, so you will want these to be in the front. If you do not want the flowering herbs to go to seed early in the summer, you must pluck off the buds. The energy used to reseed goes back into the plant and allows it to grow larger for a longer period of time.
- Buy a book about herbs and read about the habitats of each one, before you grow them.
- Make a map of your garden. With the information you discover about the height, width, and how long each herb will be in the ground, you can decide where to place them.

There is nothing I enjoy more than a stroll through my herb garden before I cook, picking the fresh leaves of my herbs for dinner. When I do this, I feel as though I have added a little something special to each meal.

Sample Herb Garden

Perennial Herbs

Parsley Rosemary Oregano Chives	Sage Thyme Mint

Annual Herbs

Sweet basil Tarragon	Dill Cilantro.

Appendix 2.A.1: Herbs and Spice

Herbs (fresh or dried)	Spices
Rubbed Thyme	Celery/Celery Seed
Oregano	Cinnamon
Cilantro	Coriander
Dill	Fresh or Ground Mustard
Sweet Basil	Garlic or Garlic Salt
Parsley	Ginger, fresh or powdered
Tarragon	Lemon Pepper Seasoning
Rosemary	McCormick Montreal Steak Seasoning
Sage	Nutmeg
	Onion or Onion Salt
	Paprika
	Peppers (fresh or ground)
	Cayenne
	Black
	Melange
	Red Pepper
	Chili
	White
	Turmeric
	Salt

Appendix 2.A.2: Other Necessities

Other Necessities	
Vinegar	
White Table	Rice Wine
Balsamic	Apple Cider
Tart Fruit Juice	
Lime	Lemon
Spirits	
Sake	Red and white wine
Oils	
Vegetable—canola, soy, corn, safflower	Sesame
Olive	Peanut
Nuts and Nut Butter	
Sesame—tahini	Peanut

Chapter 3

Other Enhancements

Preparing dinner is like painting on a canvas. Each ingredient you choose adds a special color and texture to your meal. Below, I list a few ingredients I call *enhancements*:

Peppercorns

I use some kind of crushed peppercorn in almost everything I cook. If you can afford only one kind, get black pepper. It is very important to note that some very hot peppers will completely overpower any more subtle seasoning. So, be careful.

If you would like to have a few different types, try:

- *Cayenne.* This powdery, orange-red pepper is quite hot, but wonderful for digestion. You may find varying theories on all of the other peppers, but most holistic people agree that cayenne is medicinally beneficial for your health. It will fire up any dish. The Mexicans even add this pepper to corn meal and serve it with honey. Try that for something different at breakfast. Be aware, though, there is no protein in this dish. Serve some protein links or soysage with it.
- *Red Pepper.* My father sprinkled this on any Italian dish to heat up the fare. This extra kick of hot gets addictive. Once you get used to it, everything seems bland without it.
- *Ground Melange of Whole Peppercorns.* When I buy peppercorns for my pepper mill, I always buy a melange of red, white, green,

and black peppers. If a recipe calls for pepper, this mixture will enhance it beautifully.

- *White Pepper.* Chinese cuisine uses this pepper in its white sauces. It is very nice as an alternative to black or red pepper.
- *Bottled Fresh Ground Chilis.* This is a must for cooks who love hot food. I use this in most of my broth recipes, Szechwan dishes, and Mexican foods.

Vinegar

A hypothesis: Most Asian women do not get breast cancer because of the vinegar they consume. Frequently seen in Asian cuisine, rice wine vinegar is in almost every sauce and soup.

- *Apple Cider Vinegar.* I use this most often in salads, as it comprises one-third of an Italian vinaigrette. I create flavored vinegar—such as basil, tarragon, and dill vinegar—using apple cider vinegar. Marinated vinegar adds an extra herb flavor to any fresh greens. Some health experts suggest you should only use apple cider vinegar, as it is the best for your health.
- *White Table Vinegar.* This is my least favorite because of its lack of taste. I rarely use it, unless a recipe specifically requires it.
- *Balsamic Vinegar.* The Mercedes of vinegar, made from cooked trebbiano grapes, slowly aged in a variety of wooden casks and usually imported from Italy, this combination of sweet, mellow, and tart tastes enhances just about anything. It is great with roasted garlic and olive oil to marinate grilled vegetables, excellent

in a vinaigrette. I also use it for marinades and in sauces. Definitely keep a bottle of this on hand.

- *Rice Wine Vinegar*. If you plan to attempt any of the Asian recipes in this book, you must purchase a bottle. This vinegar is not as tart as others, therefore making it easier to combine with herbs and spices without overpowering the dish. Hot and sour soup, garlic sauces, and cold tofu salad would not be the same without its flavor.

Fruits

- *Lemon and Lime*. Adding the juice or rind from a lemon or lime to a meal not only gives it a tart kick, but also a burst of sunlight and freshness.

Spirits

- *Red and White Wine*. Whenever I have leftovers from a bottle of white or red wine, I pour it into a jar in the refrigerator. This is what I use when I sauté something that requires wine. I also use it in pasta sauces.
- *Sake*. Basically rice wine, this spirit tastes a lot like vodka. This is used quite frequently in Japanese cooking, so I keep a cheap bottle in the refrigerator. You can also use rice cooking wine instead of sake.

Oils

- *Olive Oil*. If I could only have one oil, it would be cholesterol-free olive oil, primarily for health reasons. Low in saturated fat, it certainly adds a rich, robust flavor to everything you cook. One draw back exists though: you cannot use olive oil to fry something sweet or something with subtle flavors. It will overtake the tastes. Otherwise, I use it in salad dressings, sauces, and stir-fry. I have asked around. The word in the Oriental chef circuits is to use olive oil—not sesame oil for stir-fry! Always buy the Extra Virgin olive oil, as it is from the first press of the olives and has the most flavor. A good olive oil has a rich, dark olive color.

• *Vegetable Oils—Canola, Soy, Corn, and Safflower.* Everyone of these oils is fine to cook or fry with. They all have so little flavor, they barely add anything to your food. So, it is safe to say you can fry with them, without changing the flavor of your recipe by much. Soy, Canola, and Safflower are lower in saturated fat—1 gram per serving—than even olive oil. But corn oil has the same amount—2 grams per serving—as olive oil. I keep a bottle of one of these oils handy to fry potatoes, plantains, and the occasional deep fry.

• *Butter.* I will not even grace this page with the option of margarine. I cannot imagine using it, not because I am a prude, but because it has so little flavor compared to butter. Recent medical studies have proven that margarine is worse for you than butter. If this is true, why deprive yourself of the rich, sweet, creamy flavor of butter in your food? Just use it in moderation. I realize it is much more expensive, but treat yourself. Even though it is high in cholesterol, occasionally, I will add it to something for company. According to the 40-30-30 diet, you are still allowed to have a small amount of fat. So, sometimes I will indulge. Feel free, though, to eliminate it from any recipe if you do not want or need it in your diet.

• *Sour Cream or Yogurt.* I put both of these creamy mixtures under one heading because I use them interchangeably, depending upon how fat-conscious I am at the time. Low fat, plain yogurt is a perfect 40-30-30 balance, with 11 grams of protein,16 grams of carbohydrates and 4 grams of fat per cup, so adding it to a cream sauce in a perfectly planned dinner will not change your balance ratio. Plain yogurt is also a good and healthy substitute for mayonnaise in potato or pasta salad. Sour cream has a heavier, bolder texture, and blends better than yogurt. But the ratio of protein to carbohydrates to fat is much higher on the fat end and lower on the protein side. Sour Cream has 8 grams of protein, 8 grams of carbohydrates, and *40 grams* of fat. In my estimation, unless you are completely indulging, use the yogurt. You can barely tell the difference. Of course, if you use fat-free sour cream, you simply deal with the carbohydrate balance, not the fat. The taste of the fat-free sour cream, in my estimation, pales to regular.

- *Nut or Seed Oils—Sesame, Peanut, and Sunflower.* These oils tend to be robust and are also a little higher in saturated fat. Still, I use them in moderation, especially in Asian food. Some say a potato fried in peanut or sesame oil makes for great French fries. If you are a fried food lover, give it a try. But do not indulge too often for the sake of your cholesterol levels.

Nut Butters

- *Tahini.* Sesame butter is made from crushed sesame seeds. I use tahini a great deal in cooking. You really cannot make Mediterranean food without it. I know it is high in saturated fat— 3 grams per 2 teaspoons, but the positive side is it also has 6 grams of protein for 2 teaspoons and no cholesterol. This is a must for hummus, cold tofu salad, some salad dressings, and cold sesame noodles. Definitely get a jar of this, but make sure it is very smooth and creamy. The jars with the oil and paste separate are often hard to remix when it is time to use the tahini.

- *Peanuts and Peanut Butter.* Another excellent way to add a little protein to a vegetarian diet is to use peanut butter in some recipes to add a nutty, creamy, and even sweet flavor to a sauce. Thai cooking has many recipes with chopped peanuts; the most famous is Pad Thai.

Protein Powders and Liquids

- *Vege Fuel.* Made by TwinLab, this 100% isolated soy protein has 15 grams of protein per scoop. It is virtually tasteless, and I find it adds a creamy texture to most foods and sauces.
- *Balance 40-30-30 Drink Mix.* This complete nutritional mix comes in a variety of flavors, should be mixed with 2% milk to provide 14 grams of protein, 19 grams of carbohydrates and 6 grams of fat. It is great in a pinch. I have even used this and the Vege Fuel in Peach Brown Betty, replacing some of the flour, to add extra protein to a sweet favorite.
- *Bragg Liquid Aminos.* This is basically an organic substitute for inorganic, table salt. In an interview with the company, I discovered it has been found that when inorganic minerals are digested in the body, they find their way to the joints and tissues of the body and deposit there, later to cause heart disease and joint problems. These liquid amino acids can be used in place of soy sauce, providing less sodium, and perhaps a little less flavor. But for health reasons, I would say, get yourself a bottle and begin substituting your salt intake with this organic, digestible substance.

Where to Shop

My students call me the Cheap Chef and rightly so. I love a bargain and cannot bare to pay twice as much for something just for convenience sake.

Every large city has ethnic districts. Quite often in these areas, ethnic grocery stores crop up. Also, farmer's markets often have a wide variety of ethnic food and supplies. This is the primary place to buy your groceries. Trust me, you will pay almost double in your grocery store for things like tahini, sesame and olive oil, shitake mushrooms, chive flowers, bok choy, and the list goes on and on.

At the end of a semester, I give my students the option to go shopping with me. Every time, the students cannot believe the fun they have while saving money and treating themselves to a culture change.

Chapter 4

Basic Ideas

A few basic recipes and ideas exist that can be used in many different meals. For instance, the meat-free burger recipe can be used with tomato sauce and pasta, in stuffed peppers or cabbage, or you can change a couple ingredients and make a meat-free loaf topped with salsa. Get creative! Learn to use these basic recipe ideas to make your favorite ethnic foods without meat.

Following each recipe, I indicate a few ideas to help you get started.

Meat-free Burgers

RECIPE
Microwave for 1 minute to defrost:
1 cup Green Giant Harvest Burger

Put in food processor:
1 cup defrosted Harvest Burger
1/2 package of Yves Veggie Ground Round
(Instead: you can use another cup of defrosted Harvest Burger)
2 tablespoon crushed tomatoes
(Instead: you can use 2 teaspoons tomato paste or ketchup)
1 tablespoon green pepper
1/4 cup Romano cheese
1/2 teaspoon garlic powder
1 teaspoon frozen basil
(Instead: 1 teaspoon dried, 8 whole fresh leaves, or 1 1/2 teaspoon jarred)

2 dashes McCormick Montreal steak seasoning
1/4 cup bread crumbs
2 dashes onion salt
1/8 cup olive oil
1/4 cup egg substitute
1/8 cup chopped, fresh parsley
Dash of salt
Ground black pepper to taste

Once you combine and chop the food processed mixture, remove from the processor.

Add Italian seasoned bread crumbs until the texture of the mixture becomes dense, but moist. You may need to add about 1/2 to 3/4 cup more bread crumbs.

You can form this mixture into balls or small patties and fry in olive oil until golden brown. Then add to tomato sauce or eat Calabrese style, which is fried.

(Optional: Instead of Yves Veggie Ground Round, you can use 1/2 cup flaked TVP. Just mix flakes with 1 cup hot water to hydrate. Then let sit for 15 minutes, draining water before use.)

Other suggested uses for this recipe: meatloaf, stuffed peppers, stuffed cabbage, stuffed grape leaves, or tacos.

Herb Broth

RECIPE
Bring to boil in saucepan:

6 cups of water
1/4 grated medium-sized onion
1/2 teaspoon chopped or crushed garlic
1 tablespoon finely chopped fresh rosemary or 1/2 teaspoon rosemary powder
1/4 teaspoon chopped ginger
2 tablespoons olive oil
1/4 teaspoon chili paste—if you like hot and spicy foods, increase this measurement
1 tablespoon of chopped parsley
Salt to taste

Let simmer on low heat for 15 minutes.

Serving suggestions: Any time you need a meat broth, substitute this recipe. You can make soup; you can use this broth to cook vegetables instead of stir-frying them, to avoid large amounts of fat; or you can add yogurt and make a cream sauce for pasta.

Tip: Keep some of this frozen for quick use.

Salad

For those who need to understand step by step what to do to make a salad, read on.

Before adding dressing, a fresh salad can consist of many ingredients. Just yesterday, a friend who has an herb garden ate a salad at my home. She was surprised I put fresh herbs in my salad. I couldn't believe she would not know how wonderful some fresh oregano, thyme, and basil would taste combined with red leaf lettuce.

So, here are some options.

For the main ingredient there is lettuce. There are many different types. I have heard that iceberg lettuce is the least nutritious, so I avoid it. Go to your local grocery and see what appeals to you. Recognize, though, that there are certain types of lettuce that are inherently bitter, such as endive, dandelion, and escarole. You may only want to add a small amount of these types of greens to another milder leaf lettuce.

So, wash the lettuce and tear it into small, bite-sized pieces.

Using a metal knife will cause the lettuce to turn brown. If you are not going to use your lettuce immediately, let it soak in cold water.

Otherwise, drain the water using a salad spinner. If you do not have a salad spinner, you can place the lettuce in a clean dish towel and pat it dry.

Then add lettuce to your salad bowl.

ADDING OTHER VEGETABLES TO A SALAD. You can add one or more of the following:

Sliced cucumber	Sliced onion
Wedge shaped slices of tomato	Celery
Carrot	Raw or parboiled broccoli
Raw or parboiled asparagus	Sliced mushrooms
Artichoke hearts	Hearts of palm

Fresh herbs to add:

Chopped parsley	Oregano leaves
Basil leaves	Thyme
Scallions	Chives

Other extras:

Cubed or grated cheese—cheddar, mozzarella, feta, Parmesan, Romano, and Monterey Jack	Black olives
Green Olives	Croutons
Hot pickled pepperoncini	Bacon bits

Once you have decided on ingredients, you are ready to add a dressing.

You could, of course, buy a salad dressing. My favorite is Annie's Shitake and Sesame Vinaigrette. (In the American dishes section of this book, I included my own version of a Shitake Sesame Salad Dressing.) Still, making one is simple—especially, a basic Italian dressing.

RECIPE

Simply add dry seasoning on top of the salad:
2 dashes of garlic powder
Salt and ground pepper to taste
Dash of dried mustard
2 dashes of oregano, if you haven't used fresh
2 dashes of rubbed thyme, if you haven't already used fresh

Then drizzle an equal amount of balsamic and apple cider vinegar over the salad. Add a little more than twice as much olive oil. Example: 2 tablespoons of vinegar to 5 tablespoons of oil.

Toss.

Everyone has different taste buds. Some like more vinegar, some like less. Just remember that the ratio is about 2.5 parts oil to 1 part vinegar, and you will do fine.

(Optional: You can also add lemon juice instead of vinegar.)

Basic Sauté Starter

Most sauté dishes start with garlic and onion. Depending on the recipe, I decide the size of onion pieces. In stir-fry, I am prone to use large pieces. In fried potatoes I like small.

Begin with a small amount of olive oil in a frying pan. Turn the pan on medium high heat. Then add onion and minced garlic.

Before I begin adding other ingredients, I usually wait for the garlic to become light brown and for the onions to turn translucent.

Marinated Baked Tofu

If you desire to use tofu in place of beef or chicken, you may consider marinating , then baking it. This recipe will provide a chewy texture with a nutty flavor.

Simply cut tofu into 1/4- to 1/2-inch slices. The thinner you make the slices, the tougher the texture. Marinate in 1/2 cup soy sauce and 1 cup water overnight or for at least 1 hour.

In preparation for baking, take tofu slices and coat them with a thick layer of nutritional or Brewers yeast. Place on a cookie sheet sprayed with olive oil non-stick cooking spray.

Bake at 350° for at least 30 minutes on each side.

If you want to make your slices thicker, bake at a lower temperature for a longer period of time.

Basically, cook the moisture out of the tofu to create a chewy texture. The longer you bake it, the more it becomes like jerky. If you cook it long enough, you may not be able to chew it at all.

For readers concerned about yeast in their diets, nutritional yeast will not grow in your body like the yeast in bread. It does, however, provide some trace minerals and vitamins rarely found in other foods.

I sometimes snack on crispy baked tofu. It is a wonderful protein-enriched extra to keep in the refrigerator to add to almost any of your favorite meals.

Remember: Adding the proper amount of protein to your diet is essential for the proper metabolism of your food.

What Kind of Pasta Should I Buy?

If you use a watery sauce such as tomato, you can use any kind of pasta you want, from the thinnest vermicelli to the thickest rigatoni. It does not matter.

When you use heavier sauces, you might want to be a little more careful. For instance, if you used vermicelli noodles for a thick pesto sauce, you may end up with a pile of mush before the sauce completely covers the pasta. Where as, if you used ravioli—filled pasta—with a pesto sauce, the noodle would hold its form while you spread the sauce over the large surface of the pasta.

If you make soups, it would be important to choose a small, spoon-sized pasta such as *ditalini*, *tubettini*, or *acini de pepe*. When cooked, these pastas easily fit on a spoon.

Remember: pasta expands. When you start off with one-half cup soup noodles, you could easily end up with enough noodles for six cups of soup.

Some kitchen stores sell expandable round gadgets that gauge how much dry spaghetti to use for specific amounts of people. If you need one, buy it. Nothing's worse than having too much pasta and not enough sauce.

Below is a complete list of Italian pastas and their corresponding shapes:

Pasta Name	Shape
Acini de pepe	Small beaded soup noodles
Cappellini	Fine strands of ribbon pasta
Casareccia	Short, curled lengths of pasta twisted at one end
Cavatappi	Short, thick corkscrew shapes
Conchigliette	Little shells used for soup
Cornetti	Ridged shells
Cresti di gallo	Curved shapes
Ditali, Ditalini	Short tubes
Eliche	Loose spiral shapes
Elicoidali	Short, ridged tubes
Farfalle	Bows
Fedeli, Fedelini	Fine tubes twisted into skeins
Festonati	Short lengths, like garlands
Fettuccine	Ribbon pasta, narrower than tagliatelle
Fiochette, Fiochelli	Small bow shapes
Prezine	Broad, flat ribbons
Fusilli	Spindles, or short spirals
Fusilli Bucati	Thin spirals, like springs
Gemelli	Twins, two pieces wrapped together
Gramigna	Grass or weed, the shapes look like sprouting seeds
Lasagne	Flat, rectangular sheets
Linguini	Long, flat ribbons
Lumache	Smooth, snail-like shells, good with seafood sauces
Lumachine	U-shaped flat noodles
Macaroni, Maccheroni	Long- or short-cut tubes, may be ridged or elbow shaped
Maltagliati	Triangular shaped pieces, traditionally used in bean soups
Orecchiette	Dished ear shapes
Orzi, Orzo	Tiny rice-like shapes, used in soups
Pappardelle	Widest ribbons either straight or saw-tooth-edge
Pearlini	Tiny rounds
Penne	Short, thick tubes with diagonal-cut ends
Pipe rigate	Ridged, curved pipe shapes
Rigatoni	Thick, ridged tubes
Ruoti	Wheels
Semini	Seed shapes
Spaghetti	Fine, medium, or thick rods
Spirale	Two rods twisted into spirals
Strozzapreti	Priest strangler, double twisted strands
Tagliarini	Flat ribbon, thinner than tagliatelle
Tagliatelle	Broad, flat ribbon
Tortiglione	Thin, twisted tubes
Tubetinni	Small piped pasta cut into bite-size soup noodles
Vermicelli	Fine, slender strands usually sold folded into skeins
Ziti tagliati	Short, thick tubes

Fresh Pasta

There are plenty varieties of fresh pasta in the refrigerator section of your local grocery. I recommend trying them. For about twice the cost of the dry, you can have pasta that tastes like homemade. The frozen pastas also taste fresher than the dried.

If you are industrious, the electric pasta machine market is selling its products dirt cheap. I have seen them for as low a $39 at the local discount, close-out stores.

Cooking Pasta

Boil at least 3 quarts of water in a sauce pot. Add a scant teaspoon of salt to the water to increase the boiling temperature and to add a little flavor. I usually start out with hot water to decrease the boiling time. Starting with cold water is supposed to be healthier, because the water has not been sitting in your hot water heater collecting whatever water collects when it sits too long. Either way, boiling it will take care of germs and molds.

When the water comes to a rapid boil, submerge all the pasta in the water. There is nothing that irritates me more than to watch someone place spaghetti in a pan of boiling water with half of it sticking out of the pan. Then our cook wonders why half of the pasta is over-cooked and the other half is not cooked enough.

My mother and aunts always break their dry pasta in half, so all of the pasta would be in the water at the same time. Take a tip from them. This also decreases the length of long pasta, making it easier to twist on to your fork.

Let the water boil while stirring the pasta almost constantly. Pasta sticks together and to the bottom of a pan, if it is not stirred frequently.

Check the container for an approximate cooking time and begin to check the pasta about 1 1/2 minutes before that time. I like my pasta *al dente*, which is an Italian idiom basically translated to mean "to the tooth" or a little chewy. So, I drain my pasta a little earlier than recommended.

Also, remember a sauce covers the pasta. If that sauce is already a hot liquid, such as spaghetti sauce, the pasta will cook a little more.

Remember, too, that pasta absorbs water and liquid. I leave a little water in my pasta when I drain it, because I know that the pasta will absorb all of the moisture from my sauce and make it dry. This is one thing you will have to actually do before you decide which recipes might require this technique. Remember the concept though.

Using a Pressure Cooker

For dried beans from scratch, I recommend using a pressure cooker. These pots used to be very dangerous. The newest versions are extremely safe and easy to use; however, they are pricey.

Of course, read the instructions. Recognize that you can cut your cooking time by two hours when you cook beans. If you are busy, that is worth the extra cost of this pot. And a stainless steel pressure cooker lasts practically forever, so it is a long-term investment.

If you put the beans directly into the pressure cooker, they will stick and burn to the bottom of the pan. One trick I have learned is to place a stainless steel bowl inside the pressure cooker. Place about 1 cup of water under the bowl, and it will act as a double boiler, preventing any burning of the beans at the bottom of the pan.

Beans generally take 30-35 minutes pressure cooked on medium-high heat.

Parboiling or Blanching

Periodically, you may want to quickly cook a vegetable to seal in its flavor. You can use parboiled vegetables such as broccoli and asparagus for freezing. Parboiling works in cold pasta salad, or in other cold dishes and salads requiring vegetables.

Personally, I am not fond of raw broccoli, but I do like it parboiled or blanched, cooking it just enough for my taste. I feel the same about raw mushrooms. I will take the parboiled ones rather than the raw ones any day.

Preparing Fresh Tomatoes for Sauce

In the summer when the tomatoes start to ripen, I always save five or six very ripe tomatoes for a fresh pot of marinated, tomato-basil sauce.

The blanching technique is simple. Core your tomatoes. Set them in a bowl or pot with a lid. Pour boiling water over them to cover the tops of the tomatoes. Cover the bowl or pot with a lid for ten minutes.

Open the lid and drain off the hot water. Immediately refill the bowl with cold water to cover the tomatoes. You should see the skins pull away from the tomato almost immediately. Now you should be able to pop the skins right off the tomato. Pop the insides of the tomatoes into a sauce pot. Compost the skins. When you have completed the process for all the tomatoes, drain the excess water from the peeled tomatoes.

You have a choice at this point: squeeze the tomatoes with your hands until you have a pulpy, chunky tomato sauce or put all the tomatoes in a blender or food processor, which will produce a pink puree instead of a hearty dark red. Now use the tomatoes to make a sauce or salsa.

Chapter 5

The Stir-fry

Woks cook food at different temperatures, because the bottom of the wok gets the most heat and the sides are cooler. Vegetarians have no meat to cook, so a wok is moot. Stir-fry all your vegetables at once.

I have a large deep frying skillet in which I usually stir-fry. My students always ask me why I do not use a wok, until they see the simplicity of using a skillet.

First, cut and dice your vegetables ahead of time. Cutting the vegetables in different shapes and sizes makes the dish look interesting. For example, you may want to cut some celery in small bite-size pieces and some in long strips. With vegetables like broccoli and cauliflower, cut approximately one-inch piece.

Try peeling away the thick skin on the broccoli stems and then slicing the tender white stalk. This is definitely the best part of the broccoli, providing yet another shape for your stir-fry.

Use up to eight vegetables. Anything more might be overkill.
Always start with:

Chopped pepper	Onion
Minced garlic	Minced ginger

Plus a combination of other fresh vegetables:

Zucchini	Broccoli
Bok choy—Chinese celery	Nappa—Chinese cabbage
Baby yellow squash	Baby yellow corn
Asparagus	Cauliflower
Green beans	Snow peas
Celery	Bean sprouts
Bamboo shoots	Water chestnuts
Mushrooms—Oyster, Portabella,	
Shitake or any exotic mushrooms	

Start with olive oil in a frying pan at medium-high heat. Add garlic, pepper, onion, and ginger—basic stir-fry ingredients.

After only two minutes, add the rest of your vegetables. The heat should be high enough to make a sizzling sound when the vegetables hit the oil. Stir them around for 3 minutes. Then add a little water, approximately1/4 cup, and place a lid on the top for 1–2 minutes.

Now season with one of the stir-fry sauces in the Chinese or Japanese sections of the cookbook.

Chapter 6

Pots, Pans, and Utensils

I am never surprised when clients and students ask me about what kind of pots and pans to purchase. Most novice cooks have absolutely no idea where to begin. Hopefully, this will give those people a jump start.

The Basics:

If you intend to cook, you must have

- A good non-stick frying pan with a lid
- 2 sauce pots—4 or 5 quarts—with lids
- A baking dish
- A plastic spatula
- A wooden stirring spoon
- A sharp paring knife
- A grater
- A colander and
- Measuring cups and spoons.

Some added extras: A good cutting board will save your countertop from nicks and cuts. You may also need a:

Blender	Cake pan
Cookie sheet	Food processor
	(I have both a small one and a
	large one)
Ladle or dipper	Large fork
Large stirring spoon with holes	Microwave
Mixing bowls	Mix-master
Omelet pan	Pasta spoon
Pizza pan	Rolling pin
Salad bowl	Small juicer
Toaster or toaster oven	Whisk for whipping and frappéing

The list can be endless. Go to your local culinary store. You will see racks and racks of gadgets and gismos designed to make your life in the kitchen easier.

My goal here is to give the beginner a place to start.

Chapter 7

Breakfast

A high protein, low carbohydrate breakfast is not generally the American way. I have eaten boxed cereal most of my life and wondered why I always felt weak with hunger two hours later. I had no energy to get me through to lunch. If you follow a high-protein diet, you have a few options. However, you will have to put most of your old ways aside.

Protein-Fortified Oatmeal

Oatmeal provides the most protein of any whole grains out there and has traces of Gamma Linolenic Acid (GLA), an essential fatty acid that makes good eicosanoids in your body. Essentially, the body needs to make good eicosanoids for you to feel energized and healthy. Aspirin helps the body to produce eicosanoids helping relieve head aches. Since these eicosanoids are drug induced, you would consider these bad eicosanoids.

RECIPE

Add one scoop of Vege Fuel plain protein powder to:
1 cup water
1/3 cup long-cooking oats
A dash of cinnamon
A dash of salt

Bring to a boil and let simmer for 5 minutes. Cover and let sit for another 5 minutes.

You can add:
1/4 cup applesauce to sweeten
Brown sugar or
Maple syrup

To add a little fat, you can add:
Milk
Almonds or
Drink a cup of low fat milk with your breakfast.
If you are not concerned about cholesterol, a little butter is nice for flavor.

Quick Cold Cereal

Most cold cereals contain little to no protein. The label of all food items should have a nutrition index. The cereal box reflects the protein, carbohydrates, and fat it provides after adding milk. Stay away from cereals that do not contain protein. The only cold cereals worth buying are made with oat bran.

The night before a breakfast of cold cereal, mix in the blender one scoop of protein powder with one cup of milk. Keep the mixture in the refrigerator overnight. Serve the cold protein-enriched milk over the cereal. This will boost your protein count.

Eggs

You can also add 1/4 cup egg substitute for 7 grams of protein to any breakfast.

Some of my favorite meat substitutes to serve with eggs in the morning are

- Morningstars Breakfast Links
- Morningstar Breakfast Patties
- Morningstar Breakfast Strips and
- Soysage—a meatloaf texture with the taste of sausage.

All the above provide various amounts of protein. Make sure you check the box for this information. Then add to these proteins one of the following:

- A piece of rye toast
- A piece of fresh fruit
- A small glass of juice
- 1/2 bran muffin or
- 1/2 bagel.

This will definitely keep you satisfied for three to four hours.

Scrambled Tofu

Tofu has 7 grams of protein per ounce. So, a breakfast with 2 ounces of scrambled tofu with a little onion, pepper, and a couple of protein links would be great with a piece of toast or half of a bagel.

Breakfast Bagel or English Muffin

Spray a large microwave-safe coffee mug with nonstick cooking spray. Scramble an egg, or use egg substitute. Place it in the mug.

Toast an English muffin or bagel.

Microwave scrambled egg for 1 to 1 1/2 minutes.

Add cheddar cheese for more protein and flavor.

Microwave a breakfast patty for required amount of time.
Place egg, cheese, and breakfast patty on bagel or English muffin.
You have your own vegetarian version of an Egg McMuffin.

Protein-Enriched Pancakes

If you feel really industrious, you can try this recipe. I have made pancakes and Morningstar Breakfast Strips a Sunday morning tradition.

Fry up all the extra pancake mix and freeze the pancakes in a sealed plastic bag. During the week, just pop one or two in the toaster for a quick meal or a dessert snack.

RECIPE

(Makes about 12-14: 4-inch pancakes)

Sift together:
1 cup presifted flour
1/2 cup Vege Fuel Protein Powder
1 teaspoon salt
3 tablespoons sugar
1 3/4 teaspoons double-acting baking powder
2 dashes cinnamon
1 dash nutmeg

Mix together:
1/2 cup egg substitute
3 tablespoons melted butter
1 1/8 to 1 1/4 cups milk

Add 3/4 of the egg mixture to the dry ingredients and mix with a fork.
Slowly add the rest of the egg mixture until you get a smooth, thick batter.
Fry in a preheated griddle or frying pan until the batter bubbles on the
upper side, before you turn the pancake. Fry it until golden brown.

Serve with jams, powdered sugar, maple syrup, or fruit syrup. Go easy
on the condiments though. Remember: Every condiment adds more carbohydrates. You should eat just one or two of these pancakes and add
some vegetable protein links or strips for more protein. I also enjoy a glass
of low-fat milk with this breakfast.

Chapter 8

Snacks

Most people need a snack between lunch and dinner and a snack later in the evening. Junk food abounds from everywhere, but what does a health-conscious person grab for a protein-enriched snack? Here are some options.

Balance or Zone Bars

These snack bars come in a variety of flavors and provide a 40-30-30 balance at 14 grams of protein per bar. My favorite flavors are Honey Peanut and Almond Brownie.

Protein Drinks

The same company that makes Balance Bars also makes Balance Protein Drinks. These come in a variety of flavors and are certainly palatable for the on-the-run person.

Edamame

If you have ever been to a Japanese restaurant and ordered Edamame, you have eaten one of my favorite snacks. These are simply boiled and salted soy beans in the pod. Upscale grocery chains now carry Edamame in the frozen food aisle. However, if you cannot find the product there, you can usually find a one pound bag of frozen soy beans in Oriental food stores for two to three dollars.

Boil 4-5 cups of water on high heat.
Place frozen soy beans in boiling water for six minutes.
Drain water and salt.

Just pop the beans from the pod directly into your mouth. This is a great night-time salty snack, instead of potato chips or popcorn.

Lupini

This Italian bean is even higher in protein than soy beans. You also pop this from its pod into your mouth.

Most of the time, I do not go through all the trouble soaking and boiling these dried beans for five days as my father did. I buy them prepared in a jar. However, they are very salty. To rectify this, try emptying the bottled water from the lupini and fill the container with fresh water three days in a row, before you eat them.

You can marinate the beans Italian style by emptying the water, after the third day of soaking, and adding

1/4 cup olive oil
1/2 teaspoon garlic powder
1/2 teaspoon onion powder and
1 1/2 teaspoon dried oregano.

Marinate overnight, then eat by placing the bean in your mouth and popping the bean from its pod. This allows you to taste the marinade and the bean at the same time.

Yogurt

Low fat plain yogurt—the dairy or soy version—is the perfect 40-30-30 combination. Perfect for a snack or a quick lunch or breakfast.

Remember, if you add fruit or sugar to yogurt, you have ruined the 40-30-30 balance.

Yogurt Cheese

If you buy a large container of yogurt and the expiration date goes by too fast, try making yogurt cheese.

RECIPE

To 1 cup of yogurt, add :
1/2 teaspoon garlic powder
1 teaspoon dill
Salt to taste

Place yogurt mixture on a cheese cloth in the refrigerator overnight. Make sure you place a container beneath it to collect the water that will separate from the yogurt.

The next day you will have yogurt cream cheese. Use your imagination and create your own healthy cheeses using spices and flavoring of your own choosing.

Cottage Cheese

Low fat cottage cheese is also another 40-30-30 perfect combination. Just add a little fresh ground pepper and you're set for the perfect snack. Remember: adding fruit to this will ruin its perfect balance.

Fried Sweet Plantains

This is not a protein-balanced snack, but it sure is good.

Buy a ripe, black plantain. If you cannot find a black one, buy a yellow one and place it in a brown paper bag until it becomes black (3-5 days). Split the plantain from top to bottom and peal off the skin. Cut into 1/4 inch slices.

RECIPE

In a frying pan, add:
1 tablespoon butter or 2 teaspoons corn oil
Fry plantains until golden brown.
To caramelize, sprinkle lightly with brown sugar before you fry them.

Hummus

Use the Hummus recipe on page 162 from the Mediterranean Section of the book and place on a cracker or pita bread.

Cajun Jerky

One of my favorite protein snacks is made by Lumen foods. Most health food chains carry this soy bean product. It has 15 grams of protein in a 1.5 ounce package and tastes great. Lumen's jerky also comes in other flavors. Keep it around the house for when you are bored and just want to chew something.

Chapter 9

Recipes

I have divided these recipes into ethnic groups. At the beginning of each section, you will find

- A necessary shopping list
- Meal suggestions based on the recipes provided
- Individual recipes each containing a short explanation of its origin and some tips.

All "HOT TIPS" are identified by highlighted paragraphs.

Size Variables

Size and shape vary from vegetable to vegetable, so exact measurements do not really exist. Here are a few helpful hint to keep you on track with not-so-precise measurements:

- *Onion size:* A medium-sized onion is about the shape of a tennis ball. If you use a huge onion and the recipe calls for a 1/4 of an onion, use less.
- *Scant:* Use a little less than the amount indicated.
- *Herb and spice amount:* Start with the amount indicated and add more to taste. The amounts shown are a starting point. Everyone

has his or her own taste buds. You will know how much salt and spice and herbs to add, once you taste your food.

American Dishes

The Shopping List:

Protein Sources:

Cheddar Cheese	Dried Beans—black, red, pinto, or white
Egg Substitute	Firm Tofu
Green Giant Harvest Burger	Milk
Morningstar Breakfast Links	Morningstar Chik Nuggets
Romano Cheese	Seitan—regular or chicken-style
Sesame seeds	Vege Fuel Protein Powder
Yves Canadian-style bacon slices	

Oils, Vinegar, Sweeteners, and Sauces:

Apple cider and red wine vinegar	Balsamic vinegar
Barbecue sauce	Honey
Ketchup	Mustard
Limes	Olive, sesame, and corn oil
Soy or canola mayonnaise	Sugar
Sweet pickle relish	Tobasco
Tomato paste	

Vegetables:

Bell pepper	Broccoli
Canned diced tomato	Carrot
Celery	Chilis
Cucumber	Kale
Lettuce	Mushrooms—Shitake and regular
Olives	Onion
Potatoes	Sauerkraut
Tomato	Yellow squash

Herbs

Basil	Bay leaves
Cayenne	Cilantro
Cumin	Curry powder
Garlic	Ginger
Ground mustard	McCormick Montreal Steak Seasoning
Nutmeg	Paprika
Parsley	Rosemary
Rubbed thyme	Sage
Spike	Spike
Zantham gum	

Complex Carbohydrates:

Acini de Pepe Pasta—soup noodles	Box of Macaroni and Cheese—dry cheese mix
Bread crumbs	Rye bread
Potatoes	

Meal Ideas

- Barbecued tofu rollups and a small garden salad
- Protein-enriched premade pizza and a salad or fresh steamed vegetables
- Protein-fortified macaroni and cheese and a green salad
- Rice, beans, salsa, and a green salad
- Roasted marinated vegetables and a Morningstar Griller
- Salad with Chik Nuggets
- Snowed-over meat-free loaf, roasted carrots, and stuffed yellow squash
- Protein sausage links and potatoes topped with salsa
- Stuffed zucchini squash with a side of brown rice and tofu au gratin
- Tiger food and one piece of rye toast
- Tofu egg drop soup and a veggie burger on one piece of rye toast
- Tofu au gratin, salad, and a small baked potato
- Vegetarian Reuben and a small salad, or tofu egg drop soup
- Buddha Bowl: steamed kale, brown rice, black beans, baked tofu, and yeast gravy
- Beef-style stroganoff with a salad
- Cabbage Stew with TVP, whole wheat bread, and a salad
- Tofu burgers, rosemary potatoes, and a salad with homemade Shitake mushroom dressing

Tiger Food—10 Minute Meal
Scrambled Tofu with Vegetables
(2 Servings)

Here's a fast, tasty way to get protein. I serve Tiger Food most often at lunch or breakfast, because the texture of scrambled tofu reminds me of scrambled eggs.

High in protein because of the tofu and full of wonderful vitamins because of the fresh vegetables, this meal will provide you with plenty of energy.

RECIPE

Sauté in 2 teaspoons of olive oil:
1 teaspoon garlic
1/4 cup chopped onion
1/2 cup sliced mushrooms
1/3 cup chopped red or green bell pepper—or mixture of peppers

When mixture begins to brown, add:
1 diced tomato
8 oz of crumbled firm tofu
1 dash rubbed thyme
1 teaspoon basil
4 sprigs of fresh, chopped parsley
2 tablespoons of fresh chives or scallions

Cover and let steam for two minutes on low heat.
Top with cheddar or mozzarella cheese before serving.

Barbecue Tofu Roll-ups—10 Minute Meal
(2 Servings)

I found a version of this recipe the first time I went to Asheville, North Carolina. A highly-evolved, spiritual community, this city seemed to resonate the word vegetarian. *It is no wonder the local restaurant served a version of this treat.*

With most of my recipes, I see an idea and create my own version. When you develop your sense of taste, you recognize certain flavors and textures. Then you begin to concoct your own creations based on the theme of another. This is culinary art.

This recipe requires barbecue sauce. There are many flavors of barbecue sauce around. I recommend purchasing a bottle of the good stuff at your local, popular barbecue joint.

RECIPE

In a frying pan sauté:
1/4 cup chopped onion
1/4 teaspoon chopped garlic
1/4 cup chopped pepper—any kind
5 1/2 to 6 ounces of cubed tofu

This also works well with baked tofu, for a different texture.
Fry mixture until tofu becomes slightly brown and onions become translucent.

Add and let simmer on low:
1/4 cup cooked green peas
1/2 cup barbecue sauce

Preheat another large skillet on medium high using no oil this time. Place one large burrito-sized flour tortilla in skillet. Let brown slightly on one side and turn. Grate cheddar cheese on the top of the tortilla or use vegetable protein cheese.

Place half of the barbecued tofu mixture in the center of the tortilla.

Slide the tortilla onto plate and roll it up. Top with Maille old-style Dijon mustard. Then make your second one with the rest of the barbecue mixture.

Barbecued Seitan—10 Minute Meal
(2 Servings)

I love barbecue sauce. I realized—after I became a vegetarian—I was not craving the ribs or pulled pork, but the tangy sauce. I look for every chance I can to use barbecue sauce in a meal. This recipe is so simple and tastes so much like beef barbecue, you will not believe it.

RECIPE

In a frying pan sauté:
1/4 cup chopped onion
1/4 teaspoon chopped garlic
1/4 cup chopped pepper—any variety
8 ounces of seitan, sliced very thin

Fry mixture until seitan becomes slightly brown and onions translucent. Add 1/2 cup barbecue sauce and let simmer on low for 2 minutes. Serve hot on a whole wheat bun.

Beef-style Stroganoff
(Serves 5)

Here is a recipe that will stir your desire for food rich with taste and texture. I developed this recipe after trying TVP beef-style strips. This texture is wonderful in sauces and stews, as well as in this hearty dish.

RECIPE

In a deep skillet combine:
1 cup TVP beef style
1/2 cup wine
2 cups water
1 teaspoon chopped garlic
3/4 cup coconut milk
3/8 cup soy sauce
1/2 cup sliced mushrooms
2 teaspoons tomato paste
1 medium-sized chopped onion
1/2 teaspoon McCormicks Montreal Steak Seasoning
1/2 teaspoon rosemary powder or 1 teaspoon fresh rosemary
1/2 teaspoon dried mustard

Let simmer for 30-40 minutes, or until the TVP and onions are tender.

Just before you remove from heat, add a mixture of 1/4 cup water and 2 tablespoons of cornstarch to thicken.

Boil fettuccini or egg noodles. Serve the stroganoff over the noodles or over rice.

(Option 1: Instead of using cornstarch, thicken with 1 cup of cheddar cheese.)

(Option 2: Instead of using cornstarch, thicken with 1/2 cup sour cream.)

Tofu Burgers

This is a great high-protein, low fat recipe for someone on the go. You can make an entire batch and keep the burgers in the refrigerator for a week, or even freeze the patties to be fried or microwaved at a later time. Make sandwiches or serve with tomato sauce as a replacement for meatballs.

RECIPE

Mix in food processor:
1 cup Italian seasoned bread crumbs
1/4 cup Nutritional Yeast
1/2 grated Romano cheese
1 tablespoon fresh or dried dill
1 teaspoon dried oregano
1 teaspoon dried basil
1 teaspoon garlic powder
1 teaspoon onion powder
1 teaspoon mustard powder
1 teaspoon Montreal Steak Seasoning
1 teaspoon parsley
1/2 teaspoon ground pepper
1/2 teaspoon salt
1/2 teaspoon celery seed
2 eggs or 1/2 cup egg substitute
2 scallions (chopped)
1/2 chopped green pepper
1 tablespoon tahini
2 tablespoons ketchup
1 tablespoon soy sauce

(Optional: If you intend to use fresh herbs, add 1/8 cup fresh chopped parsley, 2 tablespoons fresh oregano, 3 tablespoons chopped basil, and 1 teaspoon dill. However, I recommend the use of powdered onion and garlic.)

Add three-quarters of a 16-ounce package of extra firm tofu to the food processor. Mix again—using the pulse mode—just until the tofu breaks up.

Take the mixture out of the food processor and place it in a mixing bowl. Mix in the last quarter chunk of tofu with hands, leaving pea-size bits of tofu in mixture.

Preheat skillet with olive oil or corn oil to fry patties.

Form patties into balls and roll in Italian-style bread crumbs. Place the balls in the hot oil, and gently press on the balls with a flat spatula to form into patties. Fry until golden brown.

Skillet Fried Potatoes with Rosemary
(Serves 3)

I was brought up on fried potatoes at least once a week. Of course, in those days, we never thought of making potatoes interesting; they were simply a staple—a way to fill our bellies. These days, I look for low fat, tasty ways to make potatoes into mouth-watering side dishes. I believe this is one simple way.

RECIPE

In a Large Skillet combine:
1 tablespoon each of corn oil, olive oil, and soy oil
4 sliced and peeled potatoes

Let fry for fifteen minutes on medium high.

Add:
1 sliced onion
1/2 teaspoon of garlic powder
1/2 teaspoon of rosemary powder
1/2 teaspoon McCormick's Montreal Steak seasoning
Ground melange of peppers to taste
Salt to taste
1/4 cup of white wine.

Cover skillet until potatoes and onions are tender.
Remove lid and let brown.

Shitake Sesame Salad Dressing

I rarely use any other salad dressing. The taste of the shitake and roasted sesame blends so beautifully together. You can replace Shoyu with regular soy sauce without much difference. You can usually find Zantham gum in a health food store. Once you have the ingredients, the recipe is simple.

RECIPE

6 tablespoons of Toasted Sesame Seeds
10 tablespoons of Shoyu
1/2 teaspoon Zantham Gum
5 medium-sized, dried, shitake mushrooms soaked in 1 1/2 cups boiling water
(Save the water from hydrating the mushrooms.)
11/2 cups shitake mushroom water
1/4 cup grape seed or olive oil
1/4 cup sesame seed oil
3/4 cup corn oil
1/2 cup apple cider vinegar
1/4 cup wine vinegar

Cabbage Stew with TVP
(Serves 5)

In the winter months I crave a hearty stew like this recipe made with Textured Vegetable Protein chunks. TVP chunks have 24 grams of protein per 1/2 cup.

You may substitute whichever vegetables are available and seasonal, but make sure you keep the cabbage, potatoes, and tomatoes. If you cook this in the pressure cooker, you can have a protein-enriched stew in less than 30 minutes from beginning to finish.

RECIPE

In a large pot or pressure cooker combine:
2 cups water
2 16 oz. cans of diced tomatoes—use fresh when seasonal
1 1/2 cups of TVP chunks (chicken- or beef-style)
2-3 cups chopped cabbage
1 diced potato
2 sliced carrots
1 large onion, diced in large chunks
1/2 green pepper, diced in large chunks
1 cup baby lima beans—frozen is fine
1/2 cup Purple Hull peas—frozen is fine

Season with:
1 teaspoon chopped garlic
1/8 cup soy sauce
1/2 teaspoon fresh ginger
1 teaspoon rosemary powder
1/4 cup hickory-smoked barbecue sauce
1/2 teaspoon red chili sauce

1 tablespoon red wine vinegar
1 teaspoon Montreal Steak Seasoning
1/8 cup olive oil
Salt and black pepper to taste

In pressure cooker, cook for 10-12 minutes after pressure builds. Or if cooking in a sauce pot, add 1 cup more water and simmer on range until vegetables become tender.

Stuffed Yellow Squash
(Serves 4)

This recipe takes the bland flavor of yellow squash to an all-time high. I have grown sage ever since I started my herb garden. But, since I have stopped eating a traditional Thanksgiving dinner with sage stuffing, I have had little use for it. Until now.

This recipe and the following recipe for stuffed zucchini combines the powerful taste of sage with the subtle taste of baby yellow squash and zucchini.

RECIPE

Slice in half, from top to bottom:
2 young yellow squash—no bigger than 6 or 7 inches long. Larger yellow squash may be bitter.

Dig out the softer, seeded center with a spoon, leaving only a 1/4" of squash as a holder for your stuffing.

In a sauté or frying pan:
Melt 2 tablespoons butter

Add:
Center of the squash
5 sage leaves—chopped finely
1/4 cup chopped celery—1 stalk with leaves
1/4 cup chopped onion
Salt and ground pepper to taste

When mixture heats and begins to fry, turn off heat.
Add 1/4 cup bread crumbs to mixture.
Restuff the squash.

Cover and bake at 350° in baking dish with 1/4 inch water at the bottom for 1/2 hour or until tender. Just before serving, uncover the top and let brown for 5 minutes.

(Optional: Add 1/4 cup finely chopped Granny Smith apple with a dash of brown sugar, for a slightly different taste.)

Stuffed Zucchini Squash with Protein
(Serves 4)

This recipe is a version of the stuffed yellow squash recipe, but adds protein and is slightly hardier, having a bit of Cajun spice added.

RECIPE

Slice one large zucchini—about 12-14 inches—in half from top to bottom.

Use a soup spoon to dig out the seeded, softer center, leaving only a 1/3" of zucchini as a holder for the stuffing. Throw out the seeds because they are too tough to use.

In a sauté or frying pan:
Melt 3 tablespoons butter

Add:
1 cup Green Giant Harvest Burger
5 sage leaves—chopped finely
1/2 cup chopped celery—1 stalk with leaves
1/2 cup chopped onion
1/4 cup chopped mushrooms
1/4 teaspoon chopped garlic—1 clove
1 teaspoon dried parsley or 1/8 cup fresh
2 dashes of cayenne
2 dashes paprika
Salt and ground pepper to taste

Simmer mixture for 5 minutes on low. Turn off heat.
Add 1/2-3/4 cup bread crumbs to mixture. The desired consistency is that of bread stuffing. Re-stuff the zucchini.

Cover and bake at 350° in a baking dish with 1/4 inch water at the bottom for 45 minutes to an hour or until zucchini is tender.

Just before serving, uncover the top and let brown for 5 minutes.

Tofu Egg Drop Soup
(Serves 4-6)

I developed this soup primarily to replace chicken- or beef-based soups. You can prepare a large pot of just the broth and freeze some in small containers for quick starts on lots of dishes.

This recipe has egg substitute in it, but you can leave it out, if you prefer. As a vegetarian, I do not have a problem with eating egg whites. Perhaps I will feel different in a year. Most cartoned egg is pasteurized, so the likelihood of getting salmonella is rare to nonexistent. In a pinch, this soup can replace an entire meal. It is rich with protein and vegetables.

RECIPE

Preparing the Herb Broth

Bring to boil:
4-6 cups of water
1/4 grated medium-sized onion
1/2 teaspoon chopped or crushed garlic
1 tablespoon fresh or dried chopped rosemary
1/4 teaspoon ginger
2 tablespoons olive oil
1/4 teaspoon chili paste—increase this if you like hot
1 tablespoon chopped parsley
Salt to taste

When water boils, add 1/2 cup *Acini de pepe* pasta or your favorite soup noodle.
Let noodles cook for 10 minutes, stirring occasionally.

Add chopped vegetables:

Small amounts of some, or each, of the following:
Broccoli, celery, carrot, spinach, bok choy, nappa

Add 1/3 block cubed tofu—5-6 ounces. Boil for another 3-4 minutes.

In a separate bowl combine:
1/4 cup egg substitute

Whisk in 2 tablespoons grated Romano cheese.

Pour mixture into boiling soup while stirring with a whisk. After one minute, take the sauce pot off of the burner.

Let stand uncovered for 2 minutes. Top with chopped scallions or chives.

(You may substitute one whole stalk of lemon grass for the rosemary, but you must heat the broth and let it simmer for 15-20 minutes to extract the flavor from the lemon grass, then continue with the recipe, disposing of the lemon grass stalk before eating the soup.)

Basic Bean Recipe
(Serves 8-10)

This recipe was taken from Hilda, an old Spanish woman I met in New York years ago. She made the best beans and rice. Over the years, the recipe has transformed to more of an American and Indian taste.

I remember the original recipe required a Mexican Adobe spice which had MSG in it, so I axed that ingredient. Also, it used callabasa, which is a Mexican sweet pumpkin that is often hard to acquire. So, I added carrot, instead. I actually like it better this way.

As your taste buds evolve, you will find you require a certain amount of flavor in food. This is a good thing. God created a vast spectrum of herbs and spices and flavors. Try each of them and get the entire human experience.

RECIPE

Place in a sauce pan:
1 lb. Beans—pinto, white, or northern
2 quarts of water

Bring water to a boil for ten minutes. Take off heat and let stand overnight—4 hours minimum. Pour off water to remove the chemical that causes excessive gas.

Add 2 quarts fresh spring or purified water to beans.

Mix in:
1 tablespoon Spike seasoning
1 large or 2 small whole onions—grated or chopped
1/4 cup olive oil
1 heaping teaspoon chopped garlic—3 whole cloves

2 stalks of celery—grated, food processed, or chopped
2 carrots—grated, food processed, or chopped
6 bay leaves
2 teaspoons of salt
1 tablespoon of honey
1/4 cup tomato paste
2 tablespoons of Balsamic vinegar
2 tablespoons of regular soy sauce
(Optional: 1/4 cup chopped cilantro)

(If you use a pressure cooker, add only 5 cups of water. Beans will take from 30 to 35 minutes. See Using a Pressure Cooker on Page53.)

Bring to a boil, then turn heat down to simmer. Beans may take up to 2 1/2 hours to get tender.

Option Two: Cook all day in a crock pot.

Serving Options: Before serving, top with one of more of the following: salsa, plain yogurt, sour cream, chopped onion, grated cheddar cheese, or black olives.

Cuban Black Beans
(Serves 8-10)

I have tasted many versions of black beans from hearty to bland. This recipe is my own and is spicy and hearty. You can eat these beans as a soup topped with a dollop of sour cream or yogurt and grated cheddar cheese. In Cuba, they serve the beans with spicy sour greens and rice.

If you choose to add rice, you may consider throwing a handful of TVP chunks in the beans to add more protein.

RECIPE

Place in sauce pan:
1 lb. Black Beans
2 quarts of water

Bring water to a boil for ten minutes. Take off heat and let stand overnight—4 hours minimum. Pour off water to remove the chemical that causes excessive gas.

Add 2 quarts fresh spring or purified water to beans.

Mix in:
1 16 oz. can of diced tomatoes
1 large or 2 small whole onions—grated or chopped
1/2 cup chopped sweet banana peppers—green or red pepper will do
1/2 cup chopped cilantro
1 tablespoon Spike seasoning
6 bay leaves
1/4 cup of regular soy sauce
2 tablespoons nutritional yeast
5 dashes Tobasco Sauce
2 juiced limes—or 1/8 cup apple cider vinegar

1/2 teaspoon cumin
1/8 cup olive oil
2 heaping teaspoons chopped garlic—3 whole cloves
1 scant teaspoon ginger
2 stalks of celery—grated, food processed, or chopped
1 carrots—grated, food processed, or chopped

(If you use a pressure cooker, add only 5 cups of water. Beans will take from 30 to 35 minutes. See Using a Pressure Cooker on page53.)

Bring to a boil, then turn heat down to simmer.

Simmering in a pot, beans may take up to 2 1/2 hours to get tender.

Option 2: Cook all day in a crock pot.

Serving Options: Before serving, top with one of more of the following: salsa, plain yogurt, sour cream, chopped onion, grated cheddar cheese, or black olives.

Salsa
(Serves 6)

This recipe should definitely be in a subheading entitled Mexican. But there is no such subheading in this book, so it comes under American. Believe me, this is very authentic and tastes better than any salsa I have ever eaten.

RECIPE

Begin with either:
1 cup chopped very ripe tomatoes
or one 15–16 ounce can diced tomatoes

Add very finely chopped:
1/8 cup onion
1/8 cup pepper—sweet bananas work great

Note: I always start with peppers that are not hot and add cayenne to increase the heat.

1 tablespoon chopped chilis
1/2 teaspoon garlic
2 dashes Tobasco
Juice of one lime
1/4 cup chopped fresh cilantro—1 tablespoon dried
1/2 teaspoon sugar
Salt to taste
Cayenne to make extra hot
Dash of cumin to taste

Try this salsa recipe over beans with a spoon of plain yogurt or sour cream.

Salad with Chick Nuggets—10 Minute Meal
(Serves 2)

Quick and tasty meals are my motto. This meal can be prepared in ten minutes, and it provides you with fresh, uncooked vegetables and protein for energy.

I use an Italian salad dressing or a shitake sesame dressing. You can also use the Japanese miso dressing for less fat or use your favorite bottled non-fat dressing.

RECIPE

Prepare 6 Morningstar Chick Nuggets per person—cooking instructions on back of box.

Chop into a large salad bowl:
Lettuce
Celery
Onion
Cucumber
Tomato
Fresh herbs—basil, oregano, thyme, chives, or parsley
(You know how much you or your family can eat.)

Mix in separate bottle or cup:
1/4 cup olive oil
1 tablespoon balsamic vinegar
1 tablespoon apple cider vinegar
1/2 teaspoon garlic salt
1 dash of rubbed thyme
1/4 teaspoon ground mustard
Ground black pepper to taste
Salt to taste

Mix desired amount of dressing into salad and toss.

Top with:
Sliced Chik Nuggets
Grated cheddar cheese
Green or black olives.

Yeast Gulch Gravy—For Buddha Bowl
(Serves 4)

You can use this gravy to replace any hearty-tasting meat gravy for mashed potatoes, rice, or meatfree loaf.

To create the Buddha Bowl, simply place steamed kale at the bottom of a large bowl. On it, place one serving of brown rice, Cuban black beans to cover, top with crispy baked tofu and yeast gulch gravy.

This is a hearty meal for a person who has been working out in the field! You might want to half the portion if you have been sitting behind a computer or knitting your dog a sweater all day.

RECIPE

Mix ingredients in blender:
1 cup water
1/2 tablespoon onion powder
1/4 cup salty soy sauce
1/2 cup nutritional or Brewers yeast
1/2 tablespoon corn or tapioca starch
2 dashes rosemary powder
2-3 dashes white pepper

Let simmer on low in a sauce pan until thick.
(Optional: Add 1 tablespoon hickory smoked barbecue sauce)

Protein Links and Skillet Fried Potatoes
(Serves 2)

Mom used to fry up potatoes about twice a week. In fact, every two weeks my family of eight went through fifty pounds of potatoes, eating them for almost every meal. So, it is safe to say, I enjoy an occasional potato meal.

Potatoes are better than rice when it comes to insulin sensitivity. Just limit the amount of potatoes and rice you eat to about a one-half cup per meal. I always try to serve complex carbohydrates in the evening because of how full and tired they make me feel.

RECIPE

In a large skillet combine:
4 teaspoons olive oil—you can decrease this
2 diced potatoes
2 chopped peppers
1 onion
1 teaspoon garlic

Sauté for 10-15 minutes, or until the potatoes become tender.
Add 8 precooked Morningstar protein links. Microwave for 1/2 the required time to defrost, then slice and add to fried potato mixture.

Add:
1 or 2 sliced green tomatoes (optional)
1/2 cup chopped celery (optional)
1/2 cup chopped carrot (optional)

Season with:
1/8 cup chopped fresh or 1 tablespoon dried parsley
Salt

Ground pepper
Cayenne

Also add fresh rosemary or basil for a different taste.

Marinated Roasted Vegetables with Grillers

I own a gas grill. In the warmer months I always crave the flavor of something grilled on the open fire. This recipe is simple. It does require, however, you have a non-stick vegetable grill attachment.

If you do not have one, you can pick one up at your local department or culinary store. You will never lose another vegetable between the grill rungs. Clean up is much easier too.

RECIPE

Prepare this dressing first:
Slow roast a bulb of garlic for one hour in your toaster oven at 275°.
When it cools, cut off the top of the garlic bulb with a sharp knife.
The cloves should pop out when you squeeze the bulb.

Place the cloves in a blender with:
1/4 cup olive oil
1/8 cup Balsamic vinegar
Coarse ground pepper and salt to taste

Blend to make a creamy dressing.

Preparing the Vegetables:
Choose vegetables such as eggplant, zucchini, squash, broccoli, cauliflower, onions, tomatoes, and peppers.

Cut or slice 1/2" thick, large portions. Toss vegetables in olive oil, salt, and ground pepper. Place on grill at medium heat.

Grill for 10 to 15 minutes, or until desired tenderness. I like my vegetables crunchier than most. You may also want to add vegetables such as broccoli, cauliflower, carrots, and eggplant, first, before vegetables like onion, peppers, and especially tomatoes, which only take a minute.

After removing vegetables from the grill, toss in the prepared dressing.

(Optional: If you do not have time to make the Balsamic-roasted garlic dressing, use a bottled Italian dressing.)

Vegetarian Reuben—10 Minute Meal
(Serves 2)

When I first had this sandwich, it was prepared with tempeh. As I have discovered that tempeh has a lot less protein than most other meat-free products, I have tried the recipe with some of the Yves sandwich products. To my delight, the sandwich tastes almost authentic.

I have a student who served it to her carnivorous parents, and they had no idea it was vegetarian. That is my kind of food!

RECIPE

Prepare 1000 Island dressing first.
Mix together in a bowl:
2 tablespoon of soy or canola egg-free mayonnaise
1/2 teaspoon sweet pickle relish
1/2 teaspoon barbecue sauce
1/2 teaspoon ketchup
1 dash of rubbed thyme

Sauté in a little vegetable oil:
1 tablespoon chopped onion
1/4 teaspoon chopped garlic
1 tablespoon chopped green or red pepper

Add one package of Yves Canadian Bacon style vegetable protein slices:
Fry for 2 minutes, flipping when brown. Melt grated cheddar or soy cheese on it. Cover and let stand off the heat.

Place 1/2 cup of canned or fresh sauerkraut in microwave for 1 minute.

On toasted rye, put 1000 Island dressing on one side and old-style Dijon mustard on the other. Put 1/2 of sauté mixture on each sandwich. Add hot sauerkraut.

Be careful to drain the water from the sauerkraut; otherwise, you will end up with a soggy sandwich.

Add tomato and serve.

Tofu Au Gratin
(Serves 4)

Though this recipe does not use cheese, the consistency reminded me of au gratin. You will not believe the simplicity of this protein-fortified recipe. If you are fond of Indian curries, this bold side dish will go well with a fresh vegetable or salad. Consider lentil soup and a small serving of pita.

RECIPE

Slice into long, thin strips:
10 ounces of tofu

Place in casserole dish.

Mix in small bowl:
4 tablespoons soy mayonnaise
1 teaspoon curry powder

Pour mixture on top of tofu.
Bake uncovered for 10-15 minutes at 350°.

Protein-Fortified Boxed Macaroni and Cheese
(Serves 3)

If you are used to the taste of boxed macaroni and cheese, the kind with the dried packet of cheese, then you should try this.

I recommend eating pasta dishes in the evening, for they tend to leave you feeling tired or groggy. If I ate this in the afternoon, I would instantly be in nap mode.

RECIPE

While boiling the recommended amount of water for your noodles, begin preparing your protein-fortified cheese mixture.

In a blender on high speed:
Combine recommended milk, butter, and cheese mix.

Add to that mixture:
1/4 cup *extra* milk
2 ounces cheddar cheese
1 scoop of Vege Fuel Protein Powder
2 dashes of rubbed thyme
1 dash of nutmeg
1/4 of a medium-sized onion
Ground pepper to taste

When the pasta becomes tender, drain off the water and put the pasta back in the hot pan.
Pour the blended cheese mixture over the pasta.

The hot pan will melt the butter and warm the milk, making it easier for the mixture to coat the pasta.

Serve warm with a fresh salad.

Snowed-Over Meat-free Loaf
(Serves 5-6)

I remember the first time I ate this dish; I was eleven years old. My neighbor Mary, who became my surrogate mother for many years, found it in a cookbook. Well, I sure did like the idea of having mashed potatoes with anything.

At that time I was already cooking for my three sisters and brother and my father, so I decided to make the meatloaf using my recipe. It was a hit. I now have the pleasure of evolving this recipe to an even higher meat-free plane.

RECIPE

Microwave for 1 minute to defrost:
1 cup Green Giant Harvest Burger

Put in food processor:
1 cup defrosted Harvest Burger
1/2 package of Yves Veggie Ground Round
2 tablespoon crushed tomatoes
(Optional: you can use 2 teaspoons tomato paste or ketchup, instead of tomatoes)
2 tablespoons green pepper
1/4 cup Romano cheese
1/2 teaspoon garlic powder
1 teaspoon frozen basil—or 1 teaspoon dried or 8 whole fresh leaves
2 dashes McCormick Montreal steak seasoning
1/4 cup bread crumbs
2 dashes onion salt
1/8 cup olive oil
1/4 cup egg substitute
1/8 cup chopped, fresh parsley
Dash of salt
Ground black pepper to taste

Once the food processed mixture becomes chopped and combined, take from the processor. Add Italian seasoned bread crumbs until the mixture becomes dense, but moist. You may need to add about 1/2–3/4 cup more bread crumbs.

Spray a baking dish or roaster with olive oil nonstick cooking spray. Form the mixture into a long oval loaf shape. Smooth the rest of your can of tomato paste—ketchup or tomatoes—on the top of the loaf.

Fill pan with 1/2 inch of water.

Serving suggestion: Around the meat-free loaf, fill pan with cut carrots, potatoes, celery, and onions.

Cover and bake for 1 hours at 350°.

Prepare 2 cups of mashed potatoes.

In a pinch, use OreIda frozen mashed potatoes. They taste almost like homemade.

Smooth mashed potatoes over the top of the meat-free loaf. Sprinkle with rosemary or parsley.

Leave baking dish uncovered and re-bake for another 15-20 minutes at 350° or until mashed potatoes brown.

Try using salsa (page 106) instead of crushed tomatoes or tomato paste.

Japanese Dishes

The Shopping List

Protein Sources:

Egg substitute Meat-free burger	Firm tofu

Oils, Vinegar, Sweeteners, and Sauces:

Brown sugar	Chili paste
Lemon juice	Miso—light, not white
Olive oil	Peanut butter
Sake	Sesame seeds
Soy sauce—double thick	Salty soy sauce
Sugar	Tahini
Tobasco	Tomato paste

Vegetables:

Bell pepper	Broccoli
Carrot	Celery
Cucumber	Frozen peas
Lettuce	Mushrooms
Onion	Seaweed (optional)
Snow peas	Sprouts
Tomato	Yellow squash

Herbs:

Cayenne	Cilantro
Garlic	Ginger

Complex Carbohydrates:

Brown rice	Medium-weight spaghetti

Meal Ideas

- Miso soup, cold sesame noodles, and baked teriyaki tofu
- Greenwich Village favorite
- Salad with baked Chik Nuggets and miso-carrot dressing
- Stir-fry with baked teriyaki tofu and brown rice
- Teriyaki seitan with stir-fry

Miso-Carrot Salad Dressing
(Serves 6)

The first time I ate at a Japanese restaurant, I remember eating the salad and drinking the remaining dressing, because it was so good. Of course, I searched everywhere and asked everyone I knew if he or she had a recipe for the dressing, but to no avail.

Then I met my Japanese neighbor Rié, who looked in her cookbooks and found something similar. At a small Japanese grocery connected to a sushi restaurant, I met the cook, who gave me the final ingredients.

The great thing about this dressing is it has little to no fat in it. Feel good about eating it.

RECIPE

Put in Blender:

1/8 of a medium onion
2 heaping teaspoons chopped ginger
1 1/2 tablespoons light, but not white Miso
1/4 cup rice wine vinegar
1 1/2 teaspoons sugar
1/2 carrot
1/8 teaspoon garlic
1/4 cup water
1 tablespoon tomato paste
2 tablespoons lemon juice or orange juice

Making the salad:

Chop:
Cucumber
Tomato
Scallions
Lettuce

You do not want to have too many vegetables or too many flavors in this salad, because of the intense ginger flavor in the dressing. Toss this salad without the dressing and serve it on the side at the table.

Miso Soup
(4 bowls)

Miso is a thick soy paste used to flavor foods and broth. A live bacteria lives in it that is excellent for digestion and for colon health. Because it is a soy product, it also has protein and has an organic salt flavor.

The key to using Miso: Never cook it in temperatures as hot as boiling water.

So, you should always whisk it in a small amount of warm water, then stir it into the soup just before serving. Should you want to rewarm the soup, never let it boil.

This recipe substitutes cilantro for the powerful tastes of fish oil and hijiki seaweed. If you add either, do not use the cilantro.

RECIPE

Place in sauce pan:
4 soup bowls of water
1/4 cup grated onion
1/8 cup chopped fresh cilantro
1/2 teaspoon chopped ginger
1/4 cup frozen peas
1/4 cup cubed tofu
Salt to taste

Optional:
2 tablespoons fish stock or fish oil
1 package dried seaweed

After the broth boils, reduce heat to simmer, cover, and let steep for 10 minutes.

With some of the broth, whisk in 2 tablespoon brown Miso.

Add Miso to broth.

Serve topped with chopped scallions or chives.

For a hardier Miso soup, you can add soup noodles or chopped vegetables such as carrots, celery, bok choy, snow peas, or cabbage.

Cold Sechzwan Sesame Noodles
(Serves 4)

I moved to New York City just out of college. Like a kid at an amusement park, I wanted to try everything. I moved into Hell's Kitchen next to a great Chinese restaurant, West Side Cottage. I tasted my first bowl of cold sesame noodles there.

If you have never tried these noodles, you are in for a taste treat. This dish has some protein from the pasta, sesame, and peanut products, but I recommend you serve it with a salad and marinated baked tofu with a teriyaki sauce.

RECIPE

Boil 9 oz. of spaghetti or ziti noodles first. (Do not use a fragile pasta. For more information about pasta sizes and shapes, see page 52.)

Drain and rinse with cold water. While in the colander, toss 2 tablespoons peanut or sesame oil into the pasta.

Let sit at room temperature to stay cool.

Chop in separate bowls:
1/2 cup thinly sliced iceberg lettuce
1 cup long thin slices of cucumber—without seeds
1/2 cup thin slices of red and green pepper
1/2 cup snow peas, sliced down the center
3 chopped scallions

Preparing the Sesame Sauce:
In cast iron or non-stick skillet slow roast: 1/2 cup raw sesame seeds with no oil in frying pan. When the first seed pops, remove the pan from the heat.

Place seeds in food processor—or use a pestle—with:
2 tablespoon of low fat peanut butter
1 tablespoon tahini

In a separate sauce pan:
Boil 2 tablespoons of Sake or rice cooking wine.
Melt in 3 tablespoons of brown sugar.
When sugar dissolves, remove from heat.

Whisk 2 tablespoons of Miso in 1/2 cup warm water.

Mix together:
Sesame seed mixture
Sake and sugar mixture
Miso
(Optional, but great: Add 1 teaspoon chili paste)

Toss this sauce into the cool pasta.
Serve pasta topped with chopped iceberg lettuce, cucumber, scallions, snow peas, and peppers.

Teriyaki Tofu
(Serves 4)

Teriyaki is one of my favorite Japanese sauces. So, when I became a vegetarian, I sincerely missed having things dressed with this sauce.

Though teriyaki tofu is not usually on a Japanese menu, you can usually request it. It is one of my favorites.

RECIPE

Marinate 10 oz. of sliced tofu in teriyaki sauce or thick sweet soy sauce overnight.

The recipe for homemade teriyaki sauce is below.

After marinating, cover tofu slices with nutritional yeast and sesame seeds.

In a baking dish coated with non-stick olive oil cooking spray, bake tofu slices for 30 minutes on each side at 375°.

I enjoy baking the tofu a little longer until it becomes chewy and a little crisp. Use the leftovers for a cold snack later.

Teriyaki Sauce

Mix in small sauce pan:
3 tablespoon double thick soy sauce
2 tablespoons Sake or rice wine
2 teaspoons light brown sugar

Heat until sugar dissolves. Remove from heat.

Stir-fry (Refer to stir-fry section, page 57):

Onion	Garlic
Ginger	Peppers
And your choice of vegetables	

Two minutes before you serve:

Stir in Teriyaki sauce and prepared tofu. Cover and let steam for 2 minutes.

Serve hot with a small serving of brown rice, or as is.

Teriyaki Seitan
(Serves 4)

Seitan has the texture of beef or chicken, so it goes well with this teriyaki sauce.

RECIPE

Slice seitan into strips and marinate in teriyaki sauce or thick sweet soy sauce for at least one hour. The recipe for homemade teriyaki sauce is on page130.

Stir-fry (Refer to stir-fry section, page 57):

Onion	Garlic
Ginger	Peppers
And your choice of vegetables	

Add marinated seitan to the vegetables. You can choose to brown this with the onions and garlic, before you add the vegetables, but seitan tends to get a little chewy, if you cook it too long.

Two minutes before you serve:
Stir in Teriyaki sauce

Cover and let steam for 2 minutes.
Serve hot with a small serving of brown rice, or as is.

Greenwich Village Favorite
(Serves 2)

I cannot tell you how many times I went to Greenwich Village to visit a little restaurant that served a dish similar to this. It combines vegetable protein, brown rice, cheese, and carrot-miso salad dressing in a simple, tasty way. Serve this with a side of salad for a light, protein-enriched meal that will keep you full and energetic for hours.

RECIPE

Prepare:
Miso-Carrot Salad Dressing (Page 124)
2 servings of your favorite rice
A side salad with sprouts, tomato, cucumber, onion, and lettuce.

Either bake, fry, or microwave your favorite meat-free patty. You can choose between Harvest Burger, Yves Burger, GardenBurger, Fantastic Foods Burger, Morningstars Grillers, whichever one you prefer. The preparation of these burgers only takes 1-2 minutes, so prepare this just before you serve your meal.

You may also choose to top your burger with cheese. Do this just prior to serving.

When the rice is done, place a portion on a dinner plate and surround it with the salad mixture. Top the rice with a portion of a meat-free protein burger.

Dress the entire meal with Japanese Miso salad dressing.

Italian Dishes

The Shopping List:

Protein:

Cheddar cheese	Egg substitute
Firm tofu	Kidney beans
Meat-free burger	Mozzarella cheese
Pine nuts	Romano cheese
Soy links	Yves pepperoni

Oils, Vinegar, Sweeteners, and Sauces:

Baking soda	Bragg Liquid Aminos
Chili paste	Olive oil
Pickled pepper juice	Sugar
Wine	

Vegetables:

Banana pepper	Bell pepper—red and green
Broccoli	Carrot
Celery	Crushed tomatoes—fresh or canned
Cucumber	Lettuce
Marinated artichoke hearts	Mushrooms
Olives—black and green	Onion
Potatoes	Sun-dried tomatoes
Tomatoes—ripe and fresh or canned diced	Yellow squash
Nutritional yeast	Onion salt

Herbs:

Basil	Cayenne
Chives	Dill
Garlic	Garlic salt
Ginger	McCormick Montreal Steak Seasoning
Oregano	Paprika
Parsley	Rubbed thyme

Complex Carbohydrates:

Bread crumbs	Pasta—your favorite
Premade pizza	Ravioli
Soup noodles—tubetini	Tortellini

Meal Ideas

- Agli a olia soup and a salad with meat-free balls
- Stuffed peppers, roasted carrots, and potatoes
- Ravioli with tomato-basil sauce, meat-free balls, and tossed salad
- Cold tortellini pasta salad and baked Italian tofu
- Sun-dried tomato pesto sauce on a cheese tortellini, soy links with onions and peppers, and a small tossed salad
- Sweet basil pesto on cheese ravioli, baked zucchini—from American menu—and steamed carrots
- *Pasta y faziole*, cold tomato salad, and baked Italian tofu

Agli a Olia Soup
Garlic and Oil Soup
(Serves 4)

One thing is for sure, when my dad fixed a five-quart pot of this soup, each of his six children waited anxiously to sit down to eat at least five bowls a piece. I remember the soup had so much hot pepper in it, my inner ear became hot. Now that is extreme!

As long as I can remember, this particular soup has always been a vegetarian favorite of mine.

RECIPE

Boil 10 cups of water.

Sauté in olive oil:
1 1/2 teaspoons minced garlic or 3-4 cloves
1/4 chopped medium-sized onion
1/2 stalk chopped celery
1 chopped banana pepper—green pepper will do

When onions become translucent, add:
1 teaspoon frozen or jarred basil or five fresh chopped leaves
Dash of dried oregano
2 dashes paprika
Salt and ground pepper to taste
(Optional: 1 or 2 teaspoons chili paste)

Add 1/4 cup water and let simmer.

When the 10 cups of water boil, add 1 cup small soup noodles. Cook until tender. Add sautéed mixture to pasta and water.

For protein:
Add cubed baked or unbaked tofu.

The secret ingredient:
1/8 cup pickled pepper or pepperoncini juice.
(If you do not have pickled peppers, try 1/2 teaspoon dry dill.)

Top with chopped scallions or chives just before serving.

Baked Italian-Style Tofu
(Serves 6)

You can do a lot with tofu. The baked texture—when you let it get crispy—is quite good and can be substituted for chicken in a meal.

This recipe was my father's Italian baked chicken recipe, before I gave it the vegetarian once-over. Now you can eat the flavor and texture of chicken without the guilt.

RECIPE

Slice 16 ounces of tofu into slabs 1/8-1/4" thick—length does not matter.

Remember that the thinner you slice tofu, the tougher it gets.

Marinate overnight in:
1/4 cup Bragg Liquid Aminos or 1/4 cup salty soy sauce
1 teaspoon chopped garlic
1 teaspoon olive oil
1 teaspoon onion salt
2 tablespoons Balsamic vinegar

In a pinch: leave out the marinating process all together.

Mix dry ingredients:
1/2 cup nutritional yeast
1/2 cup Italian seasoned bread crumbs

1 teaspoon garlic powder
1 teaspoon onion salt
1 teaspoon dried oregano
1 teaspoon dried basil
1 teaspoon dried parsley
1 teaspoon dried dill
1/2 teaspoon rosemary powder
1 teaspoon McCormicks Montreal Steak Seasoning
1 teaspoon dried mustard
1/2 teaspoon paprika
2 dashes cayenne pepper
Crushed melange of pepper—to taste
1/2 teaspoon salt

Drain marinade from tofu.
(Optional: Dredge with whole wheat flour. Dip in 1/2 cup egg substitute.)
Thickly coat tofu strips with the dry yeast ingredients.
Bake 45-60 minutes on a greased cookie sheet at 400° until coating becomes crispy.
You can spray the top side of the tofu with olive oil cooking spray for an extra crispy texture.

Tomato Sauce—Fresh or Cooked
(Serves 4)

My mom and all my Italian relatives do not usually make a fresh mari-nated tomato sauce. They tend to cook sauce about 3 or 4 hours, and add lots of meat for flavor. This particular sauce has the traditional Italian taste, but with a lot less saturated fat. Feel free to omit the butter and wine, but know it will not taste quite the same without it.

RECIPE

In a large 4"-deep skillet sauté:
2 teaspoons chopped garlic
1 tablespoon olive oil

When garlic turns light brown add:
1 16 oz. can diced tomatoes
1 16 oz. can crushed tomatoes
(See: Preparing Fresh Tomatoes for Sauce, page 54.)

Add:
1/3 stick butter
1/8 cup red or white wine
2 tablespoons frozen basil or 1/2 cup chopped fresh basil
1/4 cup chopped chives
1 tablespoon chopped fresh oregano or a dash of dried oregano
1/2 teaspoon McCormick Montreal Steak Seasoning
Dash of rubbed thyme
1/4 cup chopped parsley
1/8 cup Romano cheese
Crushed melange of pepper to taste

Tip: When the sauce begins to steam, reduce the heat to low and taste the sauce. If it is too tart or acidic, add 1/4 teaspoon of baking soda. The top of the sauce will froth for a moment, as the soda eats away the acid.

Then taste the sauce to see how much sugar and salt to add. Add 1/4 teaspoon at a time of each. Use your own judgement. Sometimes after adding the baking soda, I find the sauce does not need salt or sugar. Most of the time, that is not the case.

Other optional ingredients:
1 cup chopped mushrooms
1/4 cup chopped black olives

Add protein:
Great Harvest Burger
or Morningstar Breakfast Links
or baked tofu—chopped
My favorite protein to add to sauce is TVP chunks or strips

Let sauce come to a slow boil, then reduce to a simmer on the lowest heat for 1/2 hour. Sometimes I boil my water for the pasta at the same time I begin preparation for the sauce and use it before it has had time to marinate. It tastes fine, but not like it tastes when the herbs have had time to blend into the sauce.

After the sauce comes to a boil, you can let it marinate at room temperature for two to three hours, instead of letting it simmer.

If you choose to use TVP chunks or strips, you should add them dry directly to the sauce, just after you have tested it for acidity. The vegetable protein will absorb the sauce and make it taste wonderful.

Meat-free Balls
(Serves 4)

Hillary Clinton said, "It takes a village to raise a child." I think it takes a few generations of families to perfect a recipe. Each member of my family makes this meatball recipe a little differently. My vegetarian version is definitely the black sheep to the hard-core Italian cooks. But if you are not eating meat and crave Italian-style meatballs and sauce, this comes the closest.

RECIPE

Microwave for 1 minute to defrost:
1 cup Green Giant Harvest Burger
Put in food processor:
1 cup defrosted Harvest Burger
1/2 package of Yves Veggie Ground Round
2 tablespoon crushed tomatoes
(Instead: you can use 2 teaspoons tomato paste or ketchup)
1 tablespoon green pepper
3/8 cup Romano cheese
1 teaspoon garlic powder
2 teaspoons frozen basil
(Instead: 1 teaspoon dried, 8 whole fresh leaves, or 1 1/2 teaspoons jarred)
2 dashes McCormick Montreal Steak Seasoning
1/4 cup bread crumbs
2 dashes onion salt
1/8 cup olive oil
1/4 cup egg substitute or 2 eggs
1/8 cup chopped, fresh parsley
Dash of salt
Ground black pepper to taste

Once the food processed mixture is chopped and combined, remove from the processor.

Add Italian seasoned bread crumbs until the texture of the mixture is dense but moist. You may need to add about 1/2 to 3/4 cup more bread crumbs.

Form mixture into balls or patties.

Dip your fingers into a little water so the mixture does not stick to your hands.

Fry balls or patties in olive oil until brown. Then add to tomato sauce or eat Calabrese-style—fried.

To use less fat, roll mixture into balls and place on a cookie sheet sprayed with olive oil cooking spray. Bake at 400° for 15 minutes or until golden brown. You may want to flip them after 7 or 8 minutes.

I do not recommend placing this mixture directly into your sauce without frying or baking, because the balls will break up.

To add to tomato sauce, after frying or baking, place balls in a separate sauce pan and pour tomato sauce over the balls. Then warm on low for fifteen minutes to get the sauce to saturate the balls.

(Optional: Instead of Yves Veggie Ground Round, you can use 1/2 cup flaked TVP or an extra cup of Harvest Burger. Just mix flakes with 1 cup hot water to hydrate. Then let sit for 15 minutes, draining water before use.)

Sun-Dried Tomato Pesto
(Serves 4-6)

After preparing this recipe, you can place it in a freezer bag, flatten it out like a pancake, and then freeze the leftovers to be used in other recipes.

I enjoy stirring in 1/8 cup of tomato pesto into hummus. This also can be used to cover a cream cheese ball for a party. Also, I sometimes add it to a recipe that needs a little tomato-garlic kick.

If you have it in your freezer, I guarantee you will find a use for it, if nothing more than using it on your next batch of tortellini or ravioli. You definitely should add a protein dish when you serve this pasta.

RECIPE

Soak in 1 cup boiling water, then cover:
12 sun-dried tomatoes

In 2 tablespoons of olive oil, brown:
2 heaping teaspoons of minced garlic
1/4 cup pine nuts
(Instead: you may use cashews or walnuts or raw pistachios.)

When golden brown, let cool.

Remove tomatoes from water, but save the water.
Place tomatoes in food processor with garlic and nuts.

Add:
1/8 cup frozen or 1/4 cup fresh basil
1/4 cup Pecorina Romano cheese.
(Parmesan or regular Romano will do.)

To cut down on fat, you may use some of the water you saved soaking the tomatoes to thin the mixture, or for traditional texture use 1/8 cup olive oil. Food process.

Always use a heavier pasta with this sauce, so it does not break up when you toss it. Some of my favorites are tortellini, ravioli, rigatoni, ziti, and spirals.

Boil the pasta to the desired texture (consult Cooking Pasta on page 52).

Drain pasta. Toss 2–3 tablespoons butter or 2 tablespoons olive oil into pasta.

(To cut down on fat, use the rest of the tomato water.)

Toss in half of the pesto mixture. This sauce is intense. Try the pasta with just half the pesto first, then add more to taste.

Serve hot topped with more Romano cheese.

Sweet Basil Pesto
(Serves 4)

Nothing says nouveau Italian more than pesto. You can grow sweet basil in the summer in almost every climate. At the end of the season, my large variety plants are five feet tall. All summer I enjoy the rich, sweet flavor of this incredible herb in sauces and pestos.

In the winter you can also enjoy the fruits of your summer herb garden by freezing the basil. Learn to do this in the herb section of this book on page 26.

RECIPE

In a food processor or with a bowl and pestle combine:
1 cup fresh basil leaves—about 20 leaves—or 1/3 cup frozen basil
1/4 cup pine nuts
2 heaping teaspoons of garlic—4 or 5 cloves
1/4 cup Pecorina Romano cheese

Food process on high until nuts are ground.

Adding pesto to pasta:
Always use a heavier pasta with this sauce, so it does not break up when you toss it. Some of my favorites are tortellini, ravioli, rigatoni, ziti, and spirals.
After boiling the pasta, lightly toss with olive oil or butter.
Add the pesto gradually until the pasta is covered with a thin coat.
Serve hot, topped with more cheese.

..n Soy Links and Peppers
(Serves 4)

If you have ever been to an Italian street fair, you have seen the booth with the Italian sausage fried with sweet onions, peppers, and garlic. You can make this same dish with Morningstar Breakfast Links and serve it with pasta and a green salad to make a complete, protein-fortified meal.

When you fry this, you will not believe the smell it creates in your kitchen. You will think you are in Italy.

RECIPE

In a large skillet on medium heat add:
2-3 tablespoons of olive oil
1 teaspoon chopped garlic
1 whole sliced medium-sized onion
3-4 peppers—a garden variety is nice, one yellow, one green, one banana, one red
16 links of Morningstar Breakfast Links

Sauté or fry until sausage is brown and onions become translucent.

Pizzazzing a Premade Pizza—10 Minute Meal
(Topping a single-serving pizza)

To demonstrate how much the spices and toppings make the pizza, I usually buy the cheapest generic brand of pizza for my cooking class. However, I am Italian and love pizza. I spent eight years of my life in New York City eating the world's best. Given the opportunity, I will make my own crust. But in a pinch, I will create my own pizza starting with someone else's palate.

RECIPE

Sauté in a dash of olive oil:
1 teaspoon chopped fresh or frozen basil
1/4 teaspoon garlic
1/2 cup Green Giant Harvest Burger or Yves Veggie Ground Round

If you like, add a little chopped onion and pepper and let brown slightly.

Top premade pizza with:
Harvest Burger mixture
Yves pepperoni
Crumbled tofu
1/2 teaspoon of oregano

Bake as required on package.

For a quick start: place frozen pizza in microwave for one minute, then bake in oven.

Pasta y Faziole
(Serves 4-6)

Just before Dad's biweekly paycheck, our family tended to run low on food, especially meat. We used to joke and say, "How about some hot rock soup for dinner tonight?"

Beans, pasta, and tomato sauce were cheap, so most of the time we mixed up an old Italian favorite, which translates to mean noodles and beans.

You can either add a can of black, kidney, white, or pinto beans to your tomato sauce and serve it with the pasta or you can make a soup the way we used to when I was a kid.

RECIPE

In a skillet, sauté in 1 tablespoon olive oil until brown:
1/2 cup chopped onion
2 teaspoons chopped garlic—4 cloves
(Optional: 1/4 cup chopped pepper—any kind will do)

While you are sautéing:
Boil 6 cups of water in sauce pan.
Add 1 teaspoon of salt.
When water comes to a boil, add 1/2 cup soup noodles—try *ditalini.*

Let boil for 8 minutes on medium high, then turn down to simmer.

Add to boiling water:
A 16 ounce can of crushed tomatoes
Sauté mixture
1/2 can (8 ounces) beans
1 tablespoon frozen sweet basil or 4 leaves of fresh or 1 teaspoon dried
1/8 cup chopped parsley

Pinch of dried oregano

Add salt and pepper to taste.
Simmer for 15 minutes and serve topped with Romano or Parmesan cheese.

Cold Pasta Salad
(Serves 4)

Every time I want to impress dinner guests with recipes that are quick and attractive, I prepare this pasta salad. It is a simple and wonderful summer dish, filled with fresh garden herbs and vegetables.

RECIPE

Prepare 9-10 ounces fresh or frozen tortellini according to directions.
After boiling, drain in a colander.
Run cold water over the tortellini until they cool.
Place it in a large serving bowl.

Add:
2 cups parboiled broccoli or 10-12 spears of parboiled asparagus cut in quarters
8 ounce can sliced black olives
1/4 cup sliced green olives
1 jar of marinated artichokes hearts—chopped
1 package of Yves pepperoni
4 ounces cubed Mozzarella or a soy alternative
4 ounces cubed cheddar or a soy alternative
1 stalk of chopped celery
3 small or 2 large tomatoes—cubed
4 chopped scallions or chives
1/2 chopped green bell pepper
1/2 chopped red bell pepper

Add chopped herbs:
3 sprigs of fresh parsley leaves
4 leaves of fresh basil

2 sprigs of fresh dill or a dash of dried
20 leaves of fresh oregano
(Any, or all, of these herbs would be wonderful.)

The Dressing
Sprinkle on top of pasta and vegetable mixture:
1/2 teaspoon garlic powder
1/2 teaspoon onion salt
Salt and ground melange of pepper to taste
1 teaspoon dried mustard
2 dashes of McCormick Montreal Steak Seasoning

Add:
3 tablespoons apple cider vinegar
1/4 cup olive oil
1/4 cup corn or soy oil

Mix and let marinate in the refrigerate for an hour or more.
Stir before serving.
Depending on your taste, you may want to add a little more vinegar.
Also, feel free to use a bottled dressing.

Stuffed Bell Peppers
(Serves 4)

I love the taste of roasted peppers. This recipe uses the basic meat-free ball recipe and adds it to a pan full of vegetables and peppers. Consider one thing, though, when you prepare this: You can either stuff peppers from the top by coring them and taking out the centers, or you can simply cut the peppers in half, take out the insides, and stuff them. You get more stuffing in the pepper if you cut them in half. They may look nicer the first way though.

RECIPE

Mix up meat-free burger mix (page 43).

Prepare red, yellow, or green bell peppers for stuffing.

Stuff 4 whole or 6 half peppers with meat-free ball mixture.

Place in baking dish at least 1 1/2 inches deep.

Pour 1/2 of a 16 ounce can of crushed tomatoes in the bottom of a baking dish.

Pour the other 1/2 can of crushed tomatoes directly over the peppers.

Top peppers with a sprinkle of Romano cheese and ground black pepper.

Add:

1 16 ounce can water

2 tablespoons olive oil

1 tablespoon frozen basil or 5 fresh chopped leaves or 1 teaspoon dried

3 chopped parsley sprigs

Salt and ground pepper to taste

1 whole sliced medium-sized onion

1 teaspoon garlic

Stir roasting sauce.

Add other vegetables to roasted mixture:
Options:
Long 1/4 slices of potatoes
Whole or sliced carrots
Halved celery stalks
Quartered Vidalia onions

Cover and bake for 1 1/2 hours at 350°.
Just before serving, remove lid and let the tops brown for 5-10 minutes.

Mediterranean Fare

The Shopping List:

Protein:

Chick peas	Chik Nuggets
Falafel mix	Firm tofu
Lentils	Textured vegetable protein (TVP) medallions
Yogurt	Vegetable protein burger

Oils, Vinegar, Sweeteners, and Sauces:

Balsamic vinegar	Bragg Liquid Aminos
Chili paste	Lemon juice
Miso	Olive oil
Rice wine vinegar	Sesame seeds
Tahini	

Vegetables:

Bell Pepper	Carrot
Celery	Cucumber
Lettuce	Olives
Onion	Tomato

Herbs:

Cayenne	Curry powder
Dill	Garlic
Garlic powder	Ginger
Mint	McCormick Montreal Steak Seasoning
Onion powder	Parsley
Rubbed thyme	Scallions

Complex Carbohydrates:

Brown rice	Bulgar wheat (#1 or #2)
Pita bread	Rice

Meal Ideas

- Lentil soup topped with yogurt dressing, falafel, and mixed salad with tahini sauce on pita
- Morningstar Chik Nuggets and mixed salad with yogurt sauce on pita
- Falafel and tabouli and hummus on plate with yellow rice
- Falafel, tabouli, and hummus sandwich on pita
- Vegetable protein burger and a side of tabouli
- Fried TVP with tahini or yogurt sauce over rice and a side of tabouli
- Fried, crispy tofu and mixed salad with yogurt sauce on pita or over rice and a bowl of lentil soup

Lentil Soup
(Serves 4-6)

I had a friend who lived in Greece for four years. We were young artists try-ing to survive on minimum wage in New York. She often cooked this soup, because we could not afford much else. Lentil soup and a good loaf of bread from a nearby pasticceria *was as close to heaven as one could get in Astoria, which was also known as Little Greece.*

RECIPE

Soak 8 oz. of lentils in water for at least one hour.

Empty water and add 4-5 cups of fresh spring water.
(If you like thin lentil soup with more broth add 5 cups. If you like thick soup, add 4 cups.)

Add to broth:
2 tablespoons of Bragg Liquid Aminos or salty soy sauce
One grated medium-sized onion
1 stalk of celery
1/2 carrot diced small
1/4 teaspoon of chopped garlic
Ground pepper to taste
1/8 cup olive oil
Salt to taste
(optional: 1 scant teaspoon dill)

After the soup comes to a boil, reduce the heat and let simmer for 45 minutes to one hour, or until lentils become tender.

Serve with a dollop of plain yogurt, a dash of Romano cheese, a dash of nutritional yeast, or a tablespoon of the Greek cucumber yogurt dressing (page 163).

Tabouli
(Serves 4)

Tabouli is such a beautiful side dish. It looks delicious and tastes equally as good and fresh. This side dish has no protein. So, make sure you serve it with vegetable protein.

I often use tabouli to dress a falafel pita, instead of shredded lettuce and cucumber. I have been in plenty of MidEastern restaurants that have done the same.

RECIPE

Hydrate with 1 1/2 cups boiling water:
1/2 cup Bulgar wheat—finely ground #1 or #2

Cover and let soak for 15-20 minutes.

Drain excess water and pour cooked Bulgar wheat into a large salad bowl.

Add chopped herbs and vegetables:
One bunch parsley tops—about 1 cup
1/8 cup mint leaves
4 chopped scallions
1 large tomato—small cubes
(Optional: 1/2 cup cubed cucumber)

Dress salad with:
1/8 cup lemon juice
1/8 cup olive oil
Salt and pepper to taste

Mix salad and taste. You may need to add a little more lemon juice or olive oil.

Hummus
(Serves 4)

Chick peas are a wonderful source of protein—7 grams to 1/2 cup. Hummus is especially good on pita bread or on Garden Vegetable Triscuits. You can also use this bean paste to dress up a falafel or fried marinated tofu pita pocket.

RECIPE

Combine in food processor:
One 16 ounce can of chick peas—drained of water
1/2 teaspoon chopped garlic or 1 clove
3 tablespoons lemon juice
2 tablespoons tahini—sesame butter
1/4 teaspoon salt
Dash of olive oil

This is the basic recipe.
Food process until beans are completely crushed.
Garnish with fresh parsley sprigs. Make a small well in the center of the hummus and drizzle with olive oil. Sprinkle with paprika.

If you want to try a few different varieties of this recipe, try adding any of the following:
1/4 teaspoon onion salt
1/4 teaspoon curry seasoning or
1/4 cup sun-dried tomato pesto (from the Italian section of the this book on page 145.)

Cucumber Yogurt Dressing
(Serves 8)

This dressing is great on sandwiches. Traditionally, this would go over gyro meat—lamb and beef—or a spicy chicken. Make the marinated fried tofu and create your own meatless pita. You can also use Morningstar Chik Nuggets and create a pita pocket with hummus, tabouli, and this dressing. It is out of this world.
Try a dollop of this dressing on the lentil soup.

RECIPE

Puree in blender:
1/4 cup olive oil
1/2 teaspoon
chopped garlic or1 clove
1/2 teaspoon salt
1/4 cup lemon juice
2 scallions
1 cup yogurt
1 cucumber—slice in half and remove the seeds with a spoon

Blend until cucumber mixes into the yogurt.
Pour into a bowl.

Stir in, do not blend:
1 cup sour cream

Falafel
(Serves 4)

I tried making falafel from scratch, but I am here to tell you it tasted just about the same as the premade mix. Well, compared to the hassle, I have opted to use the premade mix. I have a feeling most people reading this book will agree.

Most premade falafel mixes are made simply by mixing the dried ingredients with cold water and letting the mixture stand for ten minutes. You have the option of baking, skillet frying, or deep frying, which is the traditional method, such as you would find on the streets of New York.

Any way you choose, you can make a pita pocket sandwich, using the following tahini sauce, adding tabouli, a shredded garden salad, and some Hummus. Or you can serve these chick pea patties over rice.

RECIPE

Tahini Sauce for Falafel

In blender mix thoroughly:
1 cup sesame tahini
1/2 cup water
1/2 cup lemon juice
1 1/2 teaspoons garlic or 3 cloves
1/2 teaspoon salt

Fried Marinated Greek Tofu
(Serves 4)

This is my answer to a marinated chicken substitute. If you slice the tofu in long strips and fry it for 10-12 minutes or so, it becomes tough and chewy. It even tastes great on a sandwich.

RECIPE

Cut 16 ounces of tofu into long strips.

In sealed covered bowl, marinate tofu for at least one hour:
3 tablespoons Bragg Liquid Aminos
2 tablespoons balsamic vinegar
1 teaspoon garlic powder
1 teaspoon onion powder
1 teaspoon McCormick Montreal Steak Seasoning
(If you marinate longer than one hour, place in the refrigerator.)

Drain marinade from tofu.

In skillet add:
1 tablespoon olive oil
Tofu strips
1 or 2 sliced green or red bell peppers
1 sliced medium-sized onion

Fry until tofu gets crispy brown.
Serve on pita sandwiches or over brown rice.

Fried Marinated TVP Chunks

(Serves 4)

If you want to try using Textured Vegetable Protein (TVP) chunks, this is the perfect place. These light brown round medallions of vegetable protein do great as a meat substitute.

RECIPE

Hydrate 16 chunks in 2 cups boiling water.
Cover and let stand for fifteen minutes.

You can fry them as is or marinate the chunks in a sealed covered bowl for at least one hour in:
3 tablespoons Bragg Liquid Aminos
2 tablespoons balsamic vinegar
1 teaspoon garlic powder
1 teaspoon onion powder
1 teaspoon McCormick Montreal steak seasoning

Drain marinade from chunks.

In skillet add :
1 tablespoon olive oil
TPV medallions
1 or 2 sliced green or red bell peppers
1 sliced medium-sized onion

Fry until TVP gets crispy brown.
Serve on pita sandwiches or over brown rice.
Add Hummus, salad garnish, tahini or cucumber dressing.

Tofu Salad—10 Minute Meal
(3 servings)

I never thought I would see the day when I would eat cold tofu salad. The texture was something I thought I would never ingest. But I did and I am glad I did.

This salad, in texture, is similar to egg salad and can be used for sandwiches. Its tangy flavor goes well on toast with a juicy, ripe tomato.

RECIPE

Crumble 4 to 5 ounces of firm tofu into bowl.

Mix in separate bowl:
1 tablespoon tahini
2 tablespoons rice wine vinegar
1 tablespoon miso
(Optional: 1 dash of curry powder or 1 dash rubbed thyme)

Gently stir sauce into tofu.

Add to mixture:
1/4 cup chopped black or green olives
1 chopped scallion
1/2 stalk chopped celery

Chinese

The Shopping List:

Protein:

Egg substitute	Firm tofu
Romano cheese	Sesame seeds

Oils, Vinegar, Sweeteners, and Sauces:

Bragg Liquid Aminos	Brown sugar
Chili paste	Olive oil
Rice wine vinegar	Sake
Sesame oil	Soy sauce—double thick, sweet
Soy sauce—salty	Sugar

Vegetables:

Asparagus	Bamboo shoots
Bell peppers—red and green	Black tree fungus
Bok Choy	Broccoli
Carrot	Celery
Mushrooms	Olives
Onion	Shitake mushrooms
Snow peas	Spinach
Tomato	Yellow squash
Zucchini	

Herbs:

Cayenne	Chives
Cilantro	Garlic
Ginger	Parsley
Rosemary	Scallions

Complex Carbohydrates:

Acini De Pepe Pasta—soup noodles	Box of Macaroni and Cheese—dry cheese mix
Bread crumbs	Rye bread
Potatoes	

Meal Ideas

- Hot and sour soup and stir-fry with tofu
- Egg Foo Yong and a small salad
- Tofu soup and a stir-fry with garlic sauce
- Lomein topped with a tofu stir-fry in a brown sauce
- Pot stickers, hot and sour soup, and fried crispy tofu
- Baked crispy tofu in a stir-fry with a white sauce
- Hot and sour soup, and pot stickers as a main course
- Stir fry with Morningstar Farms Chik Nuggets or one of your favorite vegetable proteins in a white sauce
- Stir fry with Seitan or fried tofu in a Kung Pao sauce

Hot and Sour Soup
(Serves 4)

When I found out that traditional hot and sour soup was made with pork blood, I was horrified. Needless to say, I quickly ended my relationship with this Asian delight and set a course to develop a vegetarian version that would suit my Epicurean taste. This version of hot and sour soup is seasoned primarily with the juice from soaking dried shitake mushrooms.

RECIPE

In saucepan, boil:
1 cup water

Add:
1 teaspoon sugar
6 dried shitake mushrooms

Pour boiling water mixture over six dried shitake mushrooms. Let soak for 15 minutes.

Remove and slice the mushrooms, saving the water and replacing it in saucepan.

Add to mushroom juice:
3 cups water
Sliced shitake mushrooms
1/2 cup sliced bamboo shoots
1 1/2 ounces cubed tofu
1/4 cup sliced canned mushrooms or fresh Monterey mushrooms
1 tablespoon black tree fungus

Season with:
2 tablespoons salty soy sauce
1/4 cup rice wine vinegar
1 teaspoon or more hot chili paste
Salt and pepper to taste

Bring to a boil. Reduce heat and let cook on medium heat for ten more minutes.

To thicken soup, in separate bowl whisk:
2 heaping teaspoons of tapioca starch into
1/4 cup warm water

Slowly add to soup. You may not need all the mixture.

(Optional: whisk in hot soup, 3 tablespoons of egg substitute)
(Optional: Add vermicelli or other noodles)

Vegetable Tofu Soup
(Serves 4-6)

This recipe uses another basic herb broth you may also use to substitute for chicken or beef broth. It is simple to make and allows for the taste of the fresh vegetables to infiltrate the broth. Sometimes my body craves simple, bland food. This is definitely the time for this delicious soup.

RECIPE

Preparing Herb Broth:
In saucepan add:
4-6 cups of water
1/4 grated onion
1/2 teaspoon chopped garlic
1 tablespoon chopped rosemary or 1/2 teaspoon rosemary powder
1 teaspoon basil
1 teaspoon chopped parsley
Salt or Bragg Liquid Aminos to taste
5-6 ounces cubed firm or baked tofu

Let simmer for a few minutes on low. Then cover and let sit for an hour to allow the herbs to mingle into the soup.

For quick soup, just move directly to the next step.

Reheat the water to a slow boil.

Add a small combination of the following or your favorite vegetables:

Snow peas	Bamboo shoots
Mushrooms—oyster and sliced canned or fresh	Water chestnuts
Chopped bok choy	

Cook for 3-4 minutes.

Serve topped with chopped chives or scallions.

(Optional: Add ramen noodles—quick cooking noodles—three minutes before serving.)

Egg Foo Yong—10 Minute Meal
(Serves 2)

Every time I show my students how to make this, they cannot believe how simple and fast it is to make. Also the presentation is beautiful.

Egg Foo Yong is basically an omelet. So, if you do not eat eggs, avoid this one. For this recipe, I use egg substitute, which is primarily made of egg whites. This Egg Foo Yong is topped with a sweet and sour sauce.

RECIPE

Preparing the sauce

In small sauce pan boil:
1/2 cup water
3 tablespoons sake or rice cooking wine
1 teaspoon white sugar
1 tablespoon dark, sweet soy sauce
Dash of salt

When mixture comes to a boil, add:
1 teaspoon tapioca starch.

Whisk to dissolve and turn off, covering to keep warm.

The Vegetable
In microwave, prepare asparagus spears. Cover and cook for 2-3 minutes.

The Omelet
In skillet, fry :
3 beaten eggs or 3/4 cup egg substitute in light cooking oil—not olive oil.

When egg is almost done, turn over once to cook inside, or simply fold and cover for a minute.

Place asparagus on the plate.

Put omelet on the top of the asparagus, or fold the omelet around the vegetables.

Top with sweet and sour sauce and chopped scallions.

(Optional: Add scrambled tofu to the omelet.)

Stir-fry
(Serves 4)

Below, I explain how to make three different sauces to add to your stir-fry. (For information about Basic Stir-fry technique, see Chapter Five, page 55.)

Each sauce has a different effect on the vegetables. Beginning with the least intrusive of the recipes, the white sauce allows you to taste more of the natural flavor of the vegetables. The brown sauce definitely becomes richer. The garlic sauce, which is hot and tangy, is my personal favorite.

RECIPE

Prepare Sauces ahead of time!

The Thickening Agent
For all sauces, whisk 2 teaspoons of corn or tapioca or corn starch in 1/2 cup warm water.

White Sauce
Just add salt and white pepper to the starch mixture before adding to vegetables.
Brown Sauce

Combine in a bowl or cup:
1 tablespoon sweet, thick soy sauce
1 tablespoon salty soy sauce
1 teaspoon sugar
3 dashes white pepper
1/2 teaspoon salt

(Optional: Add a dash of sesame oil and 1 tablespoon sesame seeds for a richer, more robust flavor.)

Garlic Sauce

Combine in cup or bowl:
2 tablespoons Lee Kum Ku Vegetarian Stir-fry Sauce with Shitake mushrooms
1 1/2 teaspoons salty soy sauce
1 1/2 teaspoons sweet, thick soy sauce
1 or 2 teaspoons chili paste
2 tablespoons rice vinegar
1 teaspoon sugar
1/2 teaspoon salt

THE STIR-FRY

Start with 1-2 tablespoons olive oil in a deep frying pan or wok.
Turn heat to medium high.

Add basic stir-fry ingredients:
2 teaspoons garlic
1/4 - 1/2 cup chopped pepper
1 chopped or sliced onion
1 teaspoon chopped ginger
After 2 minutes, add desired cut and washed vegetables from list in stir-fry section (page 57).
When vegetables are almost done, add your favorite sauce.

To Thicken:
After the sauce begins to boil, add starch mixture, a little at a time, until the sauce is the desired thickness.
Take the stir-fry off the burner and cover for 1 minute.
Serve vegetables hot and crisp.

With Tofu:
Cut firm tofu into triangles. Use 4 ounces per person.
Add to mixture one minute after you have added the vegetables.
If you prefer fried, crispy tofu, you will have to do that first, or in another skillet, frying on medium high heat until it is brown and crispy. This process takes 10-12 minutes.
If you prefer the baked texture, you will also have to prepare that prior to this recipe.

Lomein
(Serves 4)

Lomein is a particular kind of Chinese noodle, slightly thicker and tougher in texture than most Italian noodles. Basically, lomein is stir-fry with noodles. Depending on your taste, you can use any of the three stir-fry sauces in the last section.

Traditionally, I believe the brown sauce would work the best. Experimenting, though, is what makes cooking fun and exciting.

RECIPE

Make basic stir-fry using the following vegetables:

Sliced celery Mushrooms Chopped scallions	Chopped Nappa—Chinese cabbage Bean sprouts

After two minutes of frying, add:
Boiled and drained lomein noodles—according to package directions
Add brown sauce (page 176) one minute before serving.

Kung Pao Sauce
(Serves 4)

You can use this hot and spicy peanut sauce to enhance a stir fry or simply pour it over baked tofu or seitan. You can keep this sauce prepared in the refrigerator for about two weeks.

RECIPE

Mix in blender:
1/4 cup peanuts
1 heaping teaspoon low fat peanut butter
3/4 teaspoon chili paste
1 teaspoon garlic
2 tablespoons regular soy sauce
1 tablespoon sweet soy sauce
1 tablespoon sesame oil
1 teaspoon rice wine vinegar
2 heaping teaspoons ginger
1/4 teaspoon flaked red pepper
1/4 cup water
1/2 teaspoon arrowroot

For Kung Pao stir fry with seitan:
Add Kung Pao Sauce to sauté mixture—onion, scallion, seitan, and vegetables—as you would any other sauce, just before serving.

Let sit in a covered pan for one minute.

Pot Stickers
(Serves 4)

Unless you live in a large city like New York or Los Angeles, you probably do not have an Oriental restaurant in your area that serves vegetarian fried dumplings. Traditionally, pot stickers or gyoza are served as an appetizer. But I often make enough for a meal. This recipe has added tofu for protein and has a simple and fantastic sauce that will make you want to serve them often. You may use the dipping sauce for other recipes, such as cold marinated vegetables. It is exquisite.

RECIPE

The Dipping Sauce

Combine in cup or small bowl:
1 tablespoon thick, sweet soy sauce
2 tablespoons regular soy sauce
1/2 teaspoon chopped garlic
1 teaspoon chopped ginger
1 teaspoon sesame oil
1 to 1 1/2 tablespoons rice vinegar
Dash of sugar
2 teaspoons chopped chive flowers or scallions
1 teaspoon sesame seeds

Let sit for 15 minutes, so flavors mingle.

Filling

Fry in 1 tablespoon olive oil:
2 teaspoons chopped garlic

2 1/2 oz. crumbled tofu
3/4 cup chopped spinach—fresh or frozen
Salt to taste

After the garlic browns, remove mixture from the frying pan.
Place mixture in food processor.

Add to mixture:
1/4 cup Romano cheese

Food process for 1 minute or until mixture becomes a paste.
Wrap in prepared gyoza wrappers as indicated, using a pastry brush and water to help bind the dough.
Fry in hot oil with the flat end of the dumpling facing down.

When the dumplings begin to turn brown, add:
1/4 cup water

Cover and let steam for 2 minutes.
Remove cover and let water evaporate.
Fry until the bottoms are crisp.
Serve with dipping sauce.

You can also steam these dumplings to avoid the extra fat.

Chapter 10

Other Health Tips

I remain open-minded about unconventional prescriptions for health. For that reason, I have tried many alternative methods for healing the body and mind. Most of these methods have helped me call upon the Divine Healer within, instead of looking to others to heal me. I believe this is what Jesus meant when he said, "Physician, heal thyself!"

This is the most important advice: Only eat, drink, and do the things that resonate peace in your heart.

Peace begins in meditation.

I begin each day with a morning meditation lasting approximately thirty minutes. I end each day with a cleansing meditation.

Peace is where I begin to assimilate Love into my life.

If we are created in the divine image of God, then we must also be God-beings. In quietness we recognize this divinity and begin to allow it into our daily lives.

We have been taught to be rational, thinking, conscious *humans doing*. We have little knowledge about the irrational, subconscious *human beings* part of our existence.

I recently heard a story:

There was a woman of forty who asked God to show her Divine Purpose.

In that moment, her guides and angels got up from the couch, where they had been reclining for forty years and jumped to attention.

Then one angel asks the woman, "Now, do you want to leave your job, or should I get you fired!"

You see, we are generally not accustomed to listening to angels, certainly not used to listening to intuition, and definitely unaware of God's voice speaking to our hearts. When you ask for light, expect to make change in all aspects of your daily habits, which includes your diet.

You have the capacity to radiate with perfect light vibrations and in fullness on this earth. But will you take the time to investigate this divinity within?

Many are now becoming conscious of their meat-eating habits, realizing that eating flesh causes the body to vibrate at lower speeds.

After only a few months of eating a vegetarian diet, one begins to feel lighter and in harmony with the plants and animals of the earth. It is a wonderful feeling.

The need to get your body and mind in shape may accompany this new feeling of lightness. For this, I would recommend Yoga. This practice helps you assimilate the power of the life force in the breath—which is known as the pranayama; teaches you the union of the body, mind, and spirit in the *asana* stretches and exercises; then lastly, helps you develop a meditative practice, perhaps, not common to your culture and religion.

If you desire spiritual things, then put your daily life on a spiritual path of unfoldment. Constantly watch the daily metaphors of life manifesting all around you in nature. Use the irrational messages of your heart to guide you to natural herbs and homeopathic cures, instead of conventional medicine. Let the voice of Divine Wisdom, resting in your heart of hearts, lead you away from that which harms you. Let it draw you to the Loving Arms of God.

Be at peace.

Appendix

Spices by Ethnic Group

Spanish:

basil onion cilantro	bay leaf paprika—mild peppers—sweet and hot	garlic parsley saffron

East European:

caraway mushroom parsley	dill seed and weed onion poppy seed	horseradish paprika

French:

basil cloves horseradish mustard onion pepper—sweet and hot savory	bay leaf dill weed marjoram nutmeg paprika—mild rosemary tarragon	celery seed garlic mushroom nuts—almonds, walnuts parsley sage thyme

Mexican:

basil cumin oregano	chili powder garlic pepper—sweet and hot	cilantro onion

Italian:

basil	bay leaf	garlic
marjoram	mushroom	onion
oregano	parsley	pepper—sweet and hot
rosemary	saffron	thyme
tomato		

Mediterranean:

basil	cinnamon	cumin
dill weed	garlic	mint
onion	oregano	parsley
pepper—sweet and hot	rosemary	sesame tahini

Asian:

anise	cilantro—Chinese parsley	cloves
garlic	ginger	mushroom
mustard	nuts—peanuts, almonds, cashews	onion
pepper—sweet and hot	sesame seed	sea weed

Indian:

cardamom	cinnamon	cloves
coriander seed	cumin—ground or seed	dill—seed or weed
fennel seed	fenugreek	garlic
ginger	mustard seed	nuts
onion	pepper—sweet and hot	poppy seed
saffron	sesame seed	tomato
turmeric		

9 780595 132744